THE LIBRARY AND INFORMATION PROFESSIONAL'S GUIDE TO THE INTERNET

Second Edition

THE LIBRARY AND INFORMATION PROFESSIONAL'S GUIDE TO THE INTERNET

Second Edition

Gwyneth Tseng
Department of Information and Library Studies, Loughborough University of Technology

Alan Poulter
Department of Information and Library Studies, Loughborough University of Technology

Debra Hiom
Institute for Learning and Research Technology, University of Bristol

LIBRARY ASSOCIATION PUBLISHING
LONDON

Published by
Library Association Publishing
7 Ridgmount Street
London WC1E 7AE

Library Association Publishing is wholly owned by The Library Association.

First published 1996
This second edition 1997

British Library Cataloguing in Publication Data

A catalogue record for this book is available from the British Library.

ISBN 1-85604-221-9

Typeset in 11pt Aldine 401 and Avant Garde from authors' disks by Library Association Publishing.
Printed and made in Great Britain by Bookcraft (Bath) Ltd.

CONTENTS

PREFACE TO THE SECOND EDITION

The first edition was unanimously well received by reviewers and went through three reprints. This edition was prompted by changes to the resources in Part IV since the first edition was compiled, back in late 1995.

A number of types of change have been taken into account. First, the almost complete domination of World Wide Web has meant that Gopher servers, where still in existence, are not being updated. All references to Gopher servers have been removed from resource descriptions. Also taken out have been JANET addresses since X.25 traffic has been replaced by TCP/IP traffic.

Second, a number of resources have changed to a different Web server, in many cases because of a move from using a Web server belonging to some other organization to using a dedicated one. This should give longer term stability to URLs for these resources.

Thirdly, some categories of resources have had to be thoroughly revised, notably in the 'Subject Listings and Indexes' section. Since the first edition a new generation of World Wide Web search services has appeared and these needed to be added. All categories of resources have seen some resources retired and new ones brought in.

Finally, the text has been updated chiefly to follow developments in World Wide Web and also the aforementioned changes in resources.

PREFACE TO THE FIRST EDITION

Communication is a cornerstone of human society and the early 1990s have seen the take-off of a new communications phenomenon – the Internet. Internet has become the buzzword of the nineties. Open a professional journal, or the technology pages of a newspaper and the Internet is probably mentioned somewhere. Even TV and radio series have been devoted to it.

The Internet is a vast network of interconnected computers which spans the globe. Since 1987 it has seen an unprecedented growth which has far outstripped that of any other computer network in existence. At the time of writing there are nearly 16 million machines and 66 million people with at least electronic mail access to the network, and the number is growing daily. Indeed, the growth in usage of the Internet, however measured, is now so rapid that it is virtually impossible to quantify – statistics are out of date as soon as they are produced. The rate of development of new Internet products and services is simply staggering.

The Internet began life as an academic and research network, supported by US government finance, and for many academics and government sponsored researchers it has now established itself as a resource as vital to their work as the word processor, telephone or fax. It provides them with hitherto unparalleled free access to data and information in the form of databases, software, computing resources, reports, electronic texts, games and much more (as well as access to fee-based services too). But perhaps its greatest asset is the connection to millions of other users, providing the opportunities to communicate, disseminate and seek information with people across the world. In more than 186 countries, academics, scholars, researchers and students are using it, on a massive scale, to do just that.

In the early 1990s the Internet became widely available to private users and businesses in the USA, and this trend is now taking off in the UK and elsewhere. Whether or not the Internet survives this rapid commercialization in its current form, it undoubtedly offers a vision of a future in which computer mediated communication and information delivery will be as common-place in developed societies as the telephone and TV today. It is a phenomenon that simply cannot be ignored by the information and library community if it is to shape the 'Internet'[1] of the future.

But if the scale of the Internet is overwhelming, hardly less so is the variety of different types of information and communication facilities it offers and the whole new vocabulary it has spawned. Faced with a bewildering array of 'information at your fingertips' it is difficult to know where and how to begin. How do you find something that could be, almost literally, anywhere in the world? 'Cyberspace' contains a great deal of information that is of little or no value or interest to the vast majority of its inhabitants. How do you locate what is useful and relevant without wasting time searching through a morass of useless data?

We have produced this book as a launching pad into the world of the Internet for librarians and information professionals, academics and students who are new to networking. We hope too that Internet veterans will find the book a useful reference.

Part I gives a brief technical background and a history of the Internet. It explains the development of academic networking in the UK and looks at what the future may hold. Part II outlines what the Internet offers and how it can be used, concentrating on features that are likely to be of particular interest to library and information professionals. This part assumes no previous knowledge or experience of the Internet. Part III covers more advanced techniques for getting the most out of the Internet and the major tools that facilitate location and retrieval of information. Throughout, procedural instructions are purposefully kept to a bare minimum; this is not intended as a step-by-step guide to using various tools. There are so many tools and they change so fast that such coverage would be of limited use and quickly become out of date. Instead, we have attempted to provide just enough information to get started without overwhelming new users with too much, or unnecessarily duplicating what has already been published elsewhere. Since so many new terms have been coined to describe Internet facilities, we have emboldened these terms in the text as we introduce and define them.

The last major section of this book is a resource guide in which we have *very* selectively identified freely available Internet services which are either specifically aimed at the library and information community or offer good coverage of particular types of electronic information. These provide leads to electronic conferencing systems and journals, to general and subject-based collections of information, to library OPACs and information services, and to network information, training materials and software. We have also included special sections that lead to information from publishers, booksellers and the media, commercial online information retrieval services, government and related institutions, and relevant professional associations. Close to our own hearts, there is also a section on resources for library/information educators and trainers.

Unlike most of the other published Internet guides, our focus is on resources of most interest to UK readers although this does not restrict the coverage to UK materials only. To try to avoid the rapid obsolescence problem on the Internet, we have only quoted and referenced resources which, in our opinion, will be around for the foreseeable future. Resources are grouped into categories and each entry gives a short description, along with details of how to access it. Where a particular resource is available via a variety of different routes or systems, a UK or European option is presented first.

Obviously we can only give a *very* small selection from an almost incomprehensible wealth of materials. The other problem is that Internet services and facilities are changing and growing, quite literally, by the hour. That is the nature of the Internet – it would not be as exciting if it were not constantly improving and expanding. We have tried to concentrate on resources that are well-established. Where there are good 'meta-resources' or regularly updated directories or listings of electronic journals, OPACs and the like, we have pointed readers to these rather than attempting to reproduce their contents. With these as a starting point we hope that with time and enthusiasm to explore the Internet, readers will be able to hunt out and use resources for themselves. Whatever your professional interests or personal hobbies, someone else somewhere on the Internet shares them!

Gwyneth Tseng and Alan Poulter
Department of Information and Library Studies,
Loughborough University of Technology

Debra Hiom
Institute for Learning and Research Technology
University of Bristol

PART I
Networking fundamentals

Contents

INTRODUCTION TO PART I

Part I introduces the Internet – what it is and what it can be used for. It explains some of the technical terms that every Internet user needs. It outlines the history of the Internet, explains where the UK academic network, JANET, fits in and takes a glimpse at the future of networking. The user is also referred to Part IV, the resource guide, where a section on 'Networking organizations' lists some UK, European and international organizations that are good sources of up-to-date information on network developments.

Chapter 1
BACKGROUND AND HISTORY OF THE INTERNET AND UK NETWORKS

What is the Internet . . . ?

The first networks linking computers had begun to emerge as early as the 1940s. Not until the 1970s, however, did it become cost-effective and reliable for ordinary computer users to transmit data between computers over long distances. Today there are thousands of networks worldwide. Quarterman and Hoskins have identified five basic types according to their purpose and administration:[1]

- **Research or academic** – established, normally with government support, for use by members of the academic and research community. These networks generally serve a region or a country. Examples include **BITNET** in the USA and **JANET** in the UK.
- **Company** – in-house proprietary systems, linking staff and machines at a single site and/or between branches and divisions of a company or organization; these are normally private with tight security to restrict access to authorized members of the organization.
- **Co-operative** – where the costs are supported by a group of separate institutions or individuals. Many cooperative cataloguing systems, whereby member libraries could exchange catalogue records, were originally established on this basis. In contrast, FidoNet is a global network of ordinary microcomputers maintained and run by computer hobbyists. In fact, FidoNet has '**nodes**' (i.e. connection points) in more countries than the Internet!
- **Commercial** (for-profit networks) – available to the public at large, or to closed user groups, on a fee-paying basis. A prime example is CompuServe, an American network with a global user base, which has recently added a range of UK-specific information to its services in order to attract more British users.

---

1 J. S. Quarterman and J. C. Hoskins, 'Notable computer networks', *Communications of the ACM*, **29** (10), 1986, 932-71.

- **Metanetworks** – these are 'networks of networks' encompassing any or all of the above types; the Internet is a metanetwork – a vast conglomerate of interconnected computer networks that brings together people, information and computer resources across the globe.

What makes the Internet more important than any other network now in existence is its overwhelming number of users – estimated at nearly 30 million with at least a basic level of access in 1994, but growing too rapidly for meaningful estimates to be made. It is by far the world's largest metanetwork, with nothing to match it in terms of the number of sites connected and number of active users. From its genesis, its critical mass of users in the academic community was sufficient to secure its success. Now, in over 186 countries worldwide, it is available to virtually the whole academic community – staff, students and administrators alike – for no charge at point-of-use (though of course not all the facilities on the Internet are freely available). Recent 'open door' policies in several countries, allowing private individuals and organizations to make relatively low-cost connections, have established the Internet as the *de facto* standard for international networking. An estimated one-third of all homes in the USA have a PC, many of these with Internet connections. The number of commercial sites connected has now overtaken the number of academic sites. The mid-1990s saw a flood of UK companies making their first, trial Internet connections, following an inexorable trend in the USA. The UK now comes second only to the USA (though admittedly a long second) in terms of the number of host computers connected – nearly 800,000 at the beginning of 1997. Although Internet access is still restricted to the academic sector in some countries, a global user-base is now emerging which once was fragmented between a large number of disparate networks.

. . . and what does it offer?

Coupled with the growth in the number of users, the ever-increasing sophistication, reliability and speed of computer-to-computer networks has spawned a completely new form of human communication – so-called **computer mediated communication** (CMC). Whereas the telephone and the broadcast media offer one-to-one and one-to-many communication respectively, the Internet offers a new dimension, namely many-to-many communication whereby groups and individuals can communicate with each other worldwide. Although the Internet is still nowhere near as pervasive as the telephone, radio or TV, it is giving rise to a new, mass communications culture, empowering groups who share a common interest not only to communicate among themselves, but to disseminate ideas, propaganda and information to wider audiences: in effect, groups and individuals can easily become publishers, lobbyists, advertisers, retailers, consultants and more. The strong ethos of freely sharing information has, to a large extent, been responsible for the Internet's meteoric growth. Commercial systems, like CompuServe, have not grown anything like as fast and after offering their users access to free Internet resources, have had to reduce charges to compete.

The Internet today gives access to an overwhelming amount of information, data and electronic information services provided by its ordinary users. At one end of the spectrum there is the 'Games Domain' providing reviews and tips on all types of computer games, run by an aficionado at Birmingham University; at the other end, official UK government information provided by the **Central Computer and Telecommunications Authority (CCTA)** and various government departments, including for the first time in 1994, an online version of the Budget.

To give a few examples, the Internet can be used to:

- exchange personal messages with colleagues, friends or relatives at other networked sites;
- engage in group discussions, exchange information and ideas with people who share a common interest, and seek information from them;
- automatically receive information on world events, leisure interests, technical, business, professional matters by subscribing to electronic journals, conferences, newsletters and alerting services;
- look up information in reference works, databases and libraries worldwide;
- retrieve journal articles, books, computer programs and graphic images and transfer them to a personal computer;
- make use of computer facilities that are not available locally;
- browse catalogues of goods and services and make credit card purchases;
- participate in distance learning and academic conferencing;
- engage in real-time 'chat' and multi-player interactive games;
- publish information for access by other Internet users.

Virtually anyone can use the Internet to look for information with only a minute or two's training – but 'cyberspace' (as it has become known) is a vast place to wander. To use many of its facilities purposefully, it is necessary to become familiar with some basic procedures and concepts. Hence we begin with some brief information on network technology to introduce the basic jargon that everyone needs, a short historical background to the main academic networks for context, and a brief indication of the developments that are shaping the face of the Internet at the present time.

We make no apologies for over-simplifying where necessary. It is all too easy to swamp beginners with a surfeit of technical detail that will simply confuse in the early stages.

Some networking terminology explained

LANs, WANs and network connections

The two basic types of network are **local area networks (LANs)** and **wide area networks (WANs)**. A LAN links computers that are physically close to each other and usually 'hard wired' together via cables. Typically, LANs are used in single organizations at single sites. WANs, however, can cover large distances, within and beyond national boundaries; they are generally connected through telecommunications links which may use a mixture of advanced technologies such as fibre-optic cables and satellites. It is the wide area networks that are of most concern here.

Computers *handle* digital data in the form of discrete bits and bytes. Networks *transmit* data in one of two forms, either analogue (a continuous signal) or digital. Most networks, like the Internet, use dedicated digital telecommunications lines. Organizations which make heavy use of an external network may install leased telecommunications lines to provide permanent, digital links from their in-house multi-user machines or LANs to external network services. Individual and private users make a dial-up connection to an **access provider** via ordinary telephone lines. This is almost invariably an analogue connection and requires translation of data between analogue and digital forms. This translation is done by a **modem**.

Bandwidth

Dedicated network lines, especially if they are made of **optical fibre**, can handle far more data than can an ordinary telephone line, even using the latest, fastest modems. The limit on data transfer, the **bandwidth** of a telecommunications line, can still be reached even on the fastest of lines when lots of users try to move vast amounts of data. In the UK, the Internet noticeably slows down throughout the day as Americans start using it in ever-increasing numbers throughout their daylight hours.

Protocols

Networks require a common framework of routines and rules to allow computers to communicate with each other. These are called **protocols**.

Protocols are technically complex, but very simply put they specify, for example, how data are to be encoded for transmission, the physical transmission media that are allowable, the conventions for addressing items of data so that they can be delivered to the correct network destination, and the applications (the types of tasks) that are to be supported on the network.

A variety of protocol suites has emerged both in proprietary networks, as for example IBM's System Network Architecture (**SNA**) and also in academic networks with **TCP/IP** (Transmission Control Protocol/Internet Protocol) for the Internet and the **Coloured Book protocols** on the original JANET service. The **OSI (Open Systems Interconnection)** reference model, first proposed by the **CCITT** (then the **Consultative Committee on International Telephone and Telegraphy**) was an attempt to impose international standardization, but has never achieved universality. A variety of different protocols continues to proliferate, although more and more users are moving to TCP/IP.

Networks using different protocols need a method of exchanging data. This is done through **gateway** services, which effectively 'translate' data from one set of protocols to another. Some gateways are more sophisticated than others. Ideally, the user should not be aware that the gateway exists, in other words the commands and operating procedures on either side of the gateway, and the facilities offered are, from a user's point of view, identical. Such gateways are said to be **transparent** or **seamless**.

Packet switching

Most WANs (including the Internet) use **packet switching** techniques. The first to do so were **X.25** networks. A protocol breaks a message down into small **packets**. Each packet includes some of the data from the message, together with a sequence code identifying where those data fit into the complete message. Each packet also has an address of the recipient computer and an address for the sending computer. Packets are totally hidden from users.

There are many advantages to using packets. They can be routed in a variety of ways between sender and recipient computers, thus bypassing any network failures or bottlenecks. Packets can be received in any order, as the sequence codes enable the original message to be re-assembled. A recipient computer can check the sequence codes of packets it receives to work out if any have been lost. The main disadvantage of packets is that they cannot handle (easily) information that must be delivered in 'real time' (i.e. according to timing restrictions). Thus sound or video can be transmitted across networks like the Internet, but a user will notice jerkiness in playback.

7

The client/server model

Any use of a network involves at least two computers: the one the user is on, and another one that is being accessed for some purpose via the network. The user's computer may be a personal computer directly connected to the network, or a multi-user **network host** to which the user connects from their own machine which acts as a terminal. Some networks, like FidoNet, operate on the **peer-to-peer** model. This means that no one computer is more important than any other. However, most networks, the Internet among them, operate the **client/server** model. One computer, the client, on behalf of the user, requests services of another computer, the server. The speed and power of the server, and the bandwidth of the network connection, determine how quickly these services are fulfilled. At any one time a server computer can be dealing with any number of client computers. Thus server computers tend to be more powerful than client computers, whose job very often entails merely the display of data passed along from a server.

This split between client and server is matched by a split in the functions of network software. A database for example might consists of a server program, which stores and retrieves data, and a client program, which generates the requests for data and displays the results. Each part of the system can be optimized for its job. The client program, for example, might operate using a **graphical user interface** (with mouse, windows and icons), to make things easy for the user. The server program would need no such adornments. Finally, the server and client programs can run on completely different makes and types of computer, which allows the formation of heterogenous networks like the Internet, which can connect a user on an archaic IBM PC XT with a Cray supercomputer.

The development of the Internet in the USA

Essentially, the Internet is a group of networks that use the TCP/IP sets of protocols to communicate. More meaningfully, the Internet is the world's largest computer network – actually, a global network of smaller university, government, corporate and commercial networks, which are linked directly or through more-or-less seamless gateways to (originally) government-financed national 'backbone' services. As far as users are concerned, the networks function almost as though they were one. They provide a pool of resources that can be reached from anywhere in the network.

The history of the Internet is a story that has been told many times, but a brief overview is necessary to understand the character and functioning of the Internet today.

Its origins lie in **ARPANET** which was commissioned in 1969 by the US Defense Department to provide a secure communications channel for US military research which would be resilient to nuclear attack. From the outset therefore, the network was decentralized, so that it could continue to function if any part were destroyed. ARPANET proved so successful that in 1983 the military use was split off and the remaining service opened up to other researchers. At that point, ARPANET connected 60 universities in the United States, one in Norway and two in the United Kingdom. By the following year, over 1000 **host computers** were connected.

The opening up of ARPANET to a wider academic cohort coincided with the genesis of desktop computing. Network links from personal computers to campus main frames, acting as Internet hosts, were established – vastly increasing the potential user group.

As more and more institutions and networks connected to ARPANET, the term internetworking (hence, internet) evolved, but ARPANET itself soon became a bottleneck. In 1985 the National Science Foundation (NSF) organized the funding of five supercomputer centres at university sites around the USA. These supercomputers provided a new **backbone** to what was known as **NSFnet** which offered vastly improved transmission speeds, capable of handling far more data traffic. The old ARPANET was gradually phased out. In the USA, regional networks were created and linked to the backbone. NSF policy was to allow anyone with an academic or research affiliation to use the network at little or no cost – indeed, campus connections were only funded if there was a local policy to provide broad access to the network for all members of the institution.

In 1987, a contract to manage the NSFnet was awarded to **Merit Network, Inc.**, a non-profit consortium of eight Michigan universities. Funding was provided by the NSF and the State of Michigan, with commercial sponsorship for improved lines and equipment. Other national networks were encouraged to connect, and commercial users started to gain access.

Today the Internet links together national backbone services, intermediate level wide area networks (both public and private) and private institutional local area networks. Over 90 countries in the Americas, Europe, the former USSR and the Pacific Rim, as well as India and South Africa have full Internet connectivity, allowing access to the all the facilities of the Internet. Many more countries have limited connections for electronic mail only. According to estimates from Matrix Information and Directory Services Inc. (MIDS), an organization which conducts ongoing investigations into the size and shape of the Internet, there were about 13.5 million people with full Internet access and 27.5 million who could exchange electronic mail as of October, 1994.[2] In just three months to January 1995, a staggering one million new host computers were connected.

BITNET

BITNET is the other major US academic network. BITNET's original purpose was to provide an inexpensive network connection to all academic disciplines within higher education and it was BITNET that first opened up computer networking for arts and humanities disciplines and to schools and colleges in the USA. BITNET networks exist in other countries too, but they are becoming less important as more sites hook up to the Internet.

Strictly speaking, BITNET is not part of the Internet because it does not use TCP/IP protocols. Nor does it offer the complete range of Internet applications, but, like many other networks that are not yet part of the Internet, it is possible to exchange electronic mail between BITNET and Internet sites, via mail gateways.

NREN and the National and Global Information Infrastructures

The National Research and Education Network (NREN) is the proposed high speed network first introduced by the then US Senator, Albert Gore in 1990 and approved by the House of Representatives toward the end of 1991.

The speed of the NREN is eventually expected to reach 2.5 billion bits per second (2.5 gigabits). This would allow 100,000 typed pages (roughly the equivalent of the *Encyclopaedia Britannica*) to be transmitted across the USA every second. Compare this to a person's typical speed of reading (around 30 characters per second – roughly the equivalent of about 300 bits per second). The visions of the Clinton administration are for a National Information Infrastructure (NII) in which every home, business and school in the USA can eventually access the network, and a commitment from governments worldwide to create a powerful and universal **Global Information Infrastructure** (GII) with open competition enshrined in its use.

Commercialization of the Internet

Paying users needed to be brought onto the network in large numbers to help finance the considerable research and development for NII. In 1994, the NSF announced that it was awarding contracts to commercial telecommunications companies to operate four new **Network Access**

---

2   MIDS Press Release, *New data on the size of the Internet and the Matrix*, December, 1994.
    http://www.tic.com/

Points (NAPs) on the high speed backbone. Previously, the backbone was reserved for traffic from educational and research institutions, with traffic from commercial sites on the Internet being routed via private, revenue generating carriers. The NSFnet backbone was decommissioned in April 1995, entirely replacing the government sponsored service with a fully commercial system of backbones.

What commercialization will mean for existing Internet users is not yet clear. There has been no discernable impact at the time of writing although the issue has been the subject for much speculation on discussion groups across the network. In the rush to encourage private-sector involvement, the future of the public-sector infrastructure is seen to be under threat. Many people fear that usage-based fees may replace the moderate subscriptions paid by many private users and that the current flexibility of the administration and openness of the system will be undermined. The culture of the Internet is at odds with commercial realities, where information has a price tag and commercial interests need to be protected.

One particular issue which highlights the conflict between public and private interests is the furore that rages around the question of advertising via the Internet. In fact, the Internet is used for advertising and there are conventions which define what is acceptable and what is not. However, for-profit activities and extensive use of the Internet for private and personal business were originally considered to be unacceptable by the NSF – and indeed, this is still the case for those with academic accounts on the Internet. Blatant advertising is still considered to be unacceptable by many Internet users. Inevitably, though, commercial concerns will increasingly look to the Internet fraternity as a new mass market for their goods and services.

Inexorable commercialization of the Internet may seem to point to an insecure future for its hitherto open and free communications infrastructure, but that is to underestimate the critical mass that the Internet has already achieved, the commitment of its users and the extraordinary rate of development of new products and services. Wherever the balance between public and private interests eventually falls, there is every reason to believe that the Internet will have an ever-increasing impact in education, businesses and homes.

Internet culture

The Internet is unusual in that it is not centrally owned, controlled or managed. Operators of participating networks cooperate to maintain the infrastructure, with one or two steering committees to coordinate

11

improvements. The most influential of these come under the auspices of the **Internet Society**, an international body made up of volunteers. This makes for a very dynamic system which is continually offering more and better features through the efforts and contributions of its enthusiastic user community.

Possibly because of its origins in US academic and research circles, the Internet has developed into a very open, democratic system in which free speech is respected (though not protected by international law); in theory at least, every user has an equal opportunity to be heard. The Internet has spawned a culture of cooperation and low-cost exchange of ideas, data and software hitherto unknown on such a scale.

Not everything about this culture is rosy however and negative aspects (like child pornography, bomb-making instructions and sexual harassment) have been extensively reported in the media. The Internet reflects the people that use it. A handful of people use the Internet for things that the vast majority of users do not approve of. This is not a problem intrinsic to the Internet but simply brought about by the existence of anti-social individuals in society. Contrary to popular opinion fostered by the traditional media, which have yet to grasp the workings of the Internet, the Internet is not awash with illicit software, pornographic images or stolen credit card details.

The development of the Internet in the UK

JANET

JANET (Joint Academic Network) is the UK academic network. Its origins lie in several small scientific networks which were developed in the UK from the late 1960s onwards, for example, the National Physical Laboratory's network established in 1968. However, JANET's direct forerunner was the Science and Engineering Research Council Network, **SERCnet**. Many university and former polytechnic sites were connected to SERCnet through switching centres at the Rutherford Appleton Laboratory, Daresbury Laboratory and the Universities of London, Cambridge and Edinburgh.

During the 1970s the Computer Board, which funded university computing services at that time, was looking to rationalize the existing UK networks and build a national backbone service. A series of investigations resulted in the formation of the **Joint Network Team (JNT)** in 1979 to spearhead developments. SERCnet was to be used as the basis of the new network, but it also integrated other Research Council networks.

JANET was inaugurated on April 1 1984. It is now funded by the **Joint**

Information Systems Committee (JISC) of the Higher Education Funding Councils and managed by the **UK Education and Research Networking Association (UKERNA)**, which has taken over the responsibilities of the JNT.

All UK universities are connected as well as Research Council establishments and other national bodies such as the British Library, the National Library of Wales and the Imperial Cancer Research Fund. An increasing number of Colleges of Further Education are also establishing JANET links. Affiliated membership is available to tertiary-level colleges. A few commercial organizations which collaborate with academic institutions are also connected – for example, Blackwells, who handle journal subscriptions for many academic libraries. By and large, though, the JANET user-base is still very firmly centred on the UK academic community, and its purpose is to support education and research.

JANET and the Internet

The Coloured Book protocols developed for the original JANET X.25 service could not be interworked with TCP/IP, so an Internet gateway was provided at the Rutherford Appleton Laboratory with a direct fibre-optic link to NSFnet being opened in 1987.

In 1991, JANET was directly linked to the Internet via the **JANET IP Service (JIPS)**. This allows TCP/IP and X.25 data to run over the JANET backbone. Now the majority of JANET usage is IP-based.

A user's connection to the JANET X.25 service is usually provided by means of a **PAD** device, or **packet assembler, disassembler**. Users who only have X.25 cannot access all the Internet facilities.

SuperJANET

Just as the USA is seeking to upgrade its networks for high performance computing, so too is the UK. In fact, work on implementing the UK high performance academic network, SuperJANET, is well advanced. Unlike the US though, there are no plans for SuperJANET to become a commercial venture.

Funding for SuperJANET was announced at the end of 1992 (£5 million per year for four years). The aim was to upgrade transmission speeds from the maximum 2 Mbps on the JANET X.25 network to speeds of between 10 Mbps and 155 Mbps, using fibre-optic technologies. This has meant a huge investment in recabling to upgrade the existing network infrastructure – not only the backbone, but also network links right through to the user's desktop. Many of the UK universities already have

SuperJANET connections and have been upgrading their own on-site networks accordingly. Funding has also been earmarked to link the British Library Document Supply Centre.

SuperJANET will open up many opportunities for academic libraries, including rapid document delivery, new electronic and multimedia publishing and greater access to large archives of information.

Some organizations involved with networking in the UK

JUGL – The JANET User Group for Libraries

JUGL provides a discussion forum for JANET users in libraries. It organizes an annual conference, runs other meetings and training workshops, produces a newsletter and some leaflets and directories from time-to-time. Importantly, it liaises with network service providers and other relevant bodies on behalf of its membership.

NISS – National Information Services and Systems

Launched in 1988, NISS provides free networked information services to JANET users. It began by offering a gateway to other information services worldwide and a bulletin board for the exchange of information within the UK Higher Education sector. NISS services are now based on Internet search and retrieval tools, although the original versions are still maintained for X.25 users. NISS also provides information services for **CHEST**, an organization which negotiates bulk purchasing agreements with software and database suppliers on behalf of UK universities.

UKOLN – The UK Office for Library and Information Networking

Based at the University of Bath, UKOLN was established to promote strategic thinking on the use of networks by the library community. It undertakes research, and provides network services and information in the areas of networking and bibliographic data management. Now funded by JISC through its **Information Services Sub-Committee (ISSC)** and by the British Library Research and Development Department, it was founded in its present form in 1992 by a merger of the UK Office for Library Networking and the Centre for Bibliographic Management (formerly the Centre for Catalogue Research). It plays a coordinating and strategic role at the forefront of UK library and information networking. Research has included strategic assessments of UK and European library network developments and priorities. UKOLN hosts the **BUBL Information Service** which is one of the most important starting points in the UK for Internet resource discovery, especially for academic librarians and their clients.

Information from both BUBL and NISS is spotlighted several times later in the book.

The future of networking: 'Information superhighways'

Upping network transmission speeds is not merely a question of coping with an increasing number of users. Even more significantly, high-speed networks will allow the real-time transmission of **multimedia** data – voice, image and video communications as well as text. In 1994, video pictures were first transmitted across the Internet, but images require far greater network bandwidth than straight text. As the volume of multimedia traffic increases, current technologies will be inadequate – hence the pressing need to implement the so-called **information superhighways** like SuperJANET and NREN.

One initiative which could rely on high-speed networking is the **Vatican Library Project**. Only a few permits are granted each year to use the library so a sample of its printed volumes, manuscripts and artwork are being digitized for electronic distribution. This could vastly improve access to the contents of rare and fragile archives. Pilot projects on SuperJANET include networking of images of rare manuscripts, video-conferencing between a number of academic test sites and the development of an electronic journal with full-page imaging.

In the summer of 1995, JISC announced funding for a range of projects under the *Electronic Libraries Programme*. This is a direct response from the UK higher education funding bodies to exploit networking to help alleviate pressures on academic library resources as student numbers and world-wide production of information spiral inexorably upwards. **On demand publishing** projects will supply reading materials in electronic format to whole classes of students and examine flexibility of access as well as licensing and copyright arrangements. A variety of **electronic journals**, some incorporating multimedia, will be developed and investigated in terms of impact on authors and readers, the economics of publishing and so forth. **Electronic ordering** and **document delivery** services will continue to be developed in an effort to cut the cost and delivery times of interlibrary loans. Not least, some of the projects aim to enhance the awareness and expertise of academic and library staff in using network resources and exploiting them appropriately.

Many other innovative applications can be imagined which are no longer wildly futuristic. Medical students from around the country could watch operations performed by leading specialists. Surgeons could keep in touch with patients in different hospitals without having to make a personal visit on each occasion. Remote conferences, courses or meetings could be held in which participants could not only send written messages, as at present, but could see and hear each other too over video and voice links. Although there are many economic, social and legal questions that will inevitably emerge with these new applications, the future looks to be a very exciting one.

A UK national superhighway?

The cost of installing a nationwide fibre-optic network to every home, office, school and hospital in the UK would run into billions of pounds. Cable companies have made a start, but the development is piecemeal and targeted towards lucrative market sectors. The government has already been urged by an all-party committee of MPs to open the way for BT to build a national high-speed network in the UK. Unlike SuperJANET, this would be available to everyone, not just academics and researchers. The committee's recommendation was that the current entertainment restrictions on BT and Mercury, which protect cable TV companies from competition, should be removed in order for BT to generate revenue to help finance the project.

What the future holds is still very uncertain, but a vision is certainly there of converging technologies for communication, information and entertainment services to homes and offices throughout the land.

PART II
What is available on the Internet?

Contents

INTRODUCTION TO PART II

Fundamentally, the Internet provides access to **people** and to **information resources**. In Part II we look at key Internet facilities under these two broad headings after first explaining the fundamental concept of a **site**. Our intention is to help new users understand Internet facilities; hence we describe the major features, advantages and disadvantages of each as they affect Internet users generally and LIS professionals in particular. In Part III we focus more practically on effective use of facilities. Many resources are mentioned in Parts II and III. These are cited in *italics* and they are all described in more detail in Part IV, the resource guide.

Chapter 2
NETWORK SITES

Site addressing – host and domain names

People and resources on a network have to have a 'site' which is defined in terms of an address of a computer on the network. Thus people are located by the particular computer they use, and information resources by the computer on which they are stored. On the Internet, site names are made up of two parts, a **host name** (which is not always evident, for example if there is only one Internet host computer at a site) and a **domain name**. A domain name is similar to the STD or area code in a telephone number. It tells you where the computer is, and what organization owns it. A host name is an identifying name for a computer within a domain, just like a telephone number identifies an individual in a particular area. Here are some typical examples:

ukoln.bath.ac.uk
www.bbc.co.uk
suna.lboro.ac.uk

Domain names are normally in three parts and read right to left. The right hand part identifies the country of the domain. Most countries have a two-letter country code:- uk for the United Kingdom, de for Germany etc. If there is no country code, then the United States is implied although there is a 'us' code which is occasionally seen.

To the left of the country code is a code showing organization type. In the UK domain these are:

ac   for academic
co   for private company
gov for government
org for an organization not of the above types

In domains for other countries, organization type codes may vary. For example, domains in the United States use 'edu' for an academic organization, while in Australia 'ac' is used. To understand the organization type in a domain name, a little judgement is called for!

The last element in a domain name is an abbreviated name for an organization. Thus Loughborough University is abbreviated to 'lboro' and the University of Bath to 'bath'. Some organizations are recognizable, others are not.

The host name is the final element. It can be something mundane (like 'hpc' for the third Hewlett Packard minicomputer) or it can be something more memorable (like 'sloth').

There are exceptions to these conventions such as:

portico.bl.uk
pipex.net

Host and domain names together identify a computer on the Internet. An alternative form of site name which can be used is the **IP address**. This is as a string of four numbers separated by full stops (e.g. 138.38.32.45 for UKOLN). These numbers are used in the actual addressing done on the Internet and an automatic translation is done (invisibly to the user) of host and domain names into numbers.

Why are host and domain names important?

The Internet is difficult to use and understand primarily because the resources it contains have no physical presence for a user, other than on a computer screen. Host and domain names not only locate people and resources but can help the user to infer something more about new resources as they are discovered. Thus a UK television schedule provided by 'www.bbc.co.uk' (the BBC) ought to have more authority than one provided on 'nyx10.cs.du.edu', a computer (host name 'nyx10') located at the Department of Computer Studies at Denver University in the United States. This is a guiding principle, not a universal rule; there are some good sources of UK information located on computers in other countries.

Host and domain names are also useful because they give relative addresses rather than absolute ones, i.e. if a service is moved or upgraded to a different computer, its IP address will change, but its site name (unless it completely transferred elsewhere) will stay the same.

Getting a connection to a site

Internet access providers

Your organization may already provide you with Internet access (as at academic sites, for example). Alternatively you can pay a commercial Internet access provider, some of which offer low-cost connections aimed at individual users, while others specialize in linking corporate networks, with a range of options (and costs) in between.

There are a rapidly growing number of commercial providers in the UK. A listing in a book would be out of date before it was published, both in terms of the organizations included and the type of access offered by each one, so we would recommend that for the latest information you pick up one of the growing crop of Internet magazines published in the UK and look for the latest details there. Or, if you already have electronic mail, you can send a request for a current list of *UK Service Providers*.

A third option is to use a **cybercafé**, where drop-in Internet access is paid for usually by the hour. The *Internet Café Guide* will show you your nearest cybercafé.

Levels of Internet access

There are essentially three levels of access to the Internet (Figure 2.1). The most basic is to be able to send only electronic messages (e-mail) to other users on the Internet. E-mail is discussed in the next chapter.

The next level up is to be **indirectly** connected to a computer that has an Internet host and domain name. Standard dial-in connections work this way, when a user with a personal computer at home or work uses standard telecommunications software and a modem to access a computer on the Internet. The Internet host computer may be operated by a commercial Internet access provider or by your own organization. The facilities available are those provided on this particular computer service.

The final level is when the user's personal computer is itself directly connected to the Internet, so that it has its own host and domain name. This level of access is also available to dial-in users, using special communications software which can emulate an Internet link. At this level the user can use any Internet facility they want, providing they have the correct client software running on their own computer. There is a growing range of such client software, most of which is available from the sites listed in the resource guide section on 'Software'.

Access at any level can be by means of a **command line interface** (where a user has to type commands at a prompt) or a **graphical user interface** (**GUI**). The latter is easier for beginners and is rapidly becoming the norm. The former is typical of older operating systems such as **DOS** and in particular **UNIX**, which was used on the majority of computers which first made up the Internet. Just about any sort of computer sold by a computer dealer for business or home office use can be used to access the Internet.

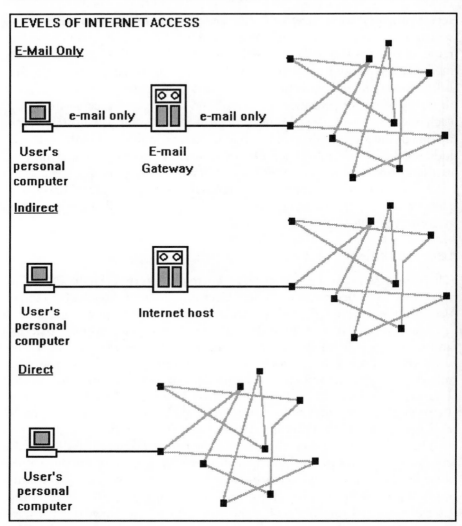

Fig. 2.1 *Levels of access to the Internet*

Password security

Whatever your level of Internet access, you will possess a **user identifier** and a **password**, which together identify you to the computer system that you use to access the Internet. Your user identifier is not secret, but your password is. Try not to write your password down in an obvious place (e.g. on a Post-It note by your computer screen). Your password should not be a word that is locatable in any sort of dictionary, nor should it be traceable to you (e.g. your car number plate). A good method of arriving at a password is to choose a phrase from a book and derive your password from its initial letters and page number (e.g. the phrase 'Is this a dagger I see before me' from page 73 of your copy of 'Macbeth' gives a password of itadisbm73). You should change your password regularly (as you come across memorable phrases in your reading!).

Chapter 3
PEOPLE

In this chapter we look at how to contact people on the Internet. Further details of the resources that are mentioned (in *italics*) can be found in the resource guide in the section on 'Discussion lists and electronic conferences'.

People – who are they . . . ?

It is virtually impossible to monitor how many people have Internet access. Some potential users never actually use their Internet connection. Other people have a number of different Internet connections. The turnover of users on some sites (e.g. at universities, when student cohorts change annually) is large. In the UK (as in most countries outside the USA) it is probably still true to say that by far the majority of users are members of the academic community, but the mid-1990s saw a massive number of non-academic institutions join the Internet, following the trend in the USA where the Internet has for several years been widely used by people in industry, commerce, government and by private citizens.

. . . and how to contact them?

Essentially there are three ways of communicating with other Internet users: **electronic mail (e-mail), electronic conferencing systems** and 'live' **interactive systems** where the participants are connected simultaneously. Electronic mail is used by individuals or groups to pass messages between each other and is available to virtually the whole Internet community. Conferencing systems allow people to contribute to a central pool of discussion on a topic; others can then selectively pick up and respond to individual messages in the pool. Live, interactive systems are used to communicate in 'real time'; in effect, participants are 'talking' rather than passing messages between each other.

Electronic mail (e-mail)

E-mail provides a fast, cheap and convenient means of passing messages between individuals and groups. For many users it is the first Internet application they come into contact with and remains the most important. Nowadays, so many other networks have e-mail gateways to the Internet that it is possible to use it to contact almost any e-mail user. Of particular note to LIS professionals, e-mail systems offered by some of the online retrieval services such as Dialog, DataStar and STN have such gateways.

E-mail addresses

On the Internet, an **e-mail address** is generally made up of three elements:

    a user identifier
    a separator character – @
    a site name

Thus examples would be:

    J.X.Smith@lboro.ac.uk
    janet-liaison-desk@jnt.ac.uk

Incoming messages go into a file called a **mailbox** on the computer identified by the host and domain name. Usually a user has their own personal mailbox, although it is possible to have a shared mailbox with other users (sales and customer support departments often do this, as in the JANET example above). A **user identifier** can be any combination of letters and numbers: it is useful to have a user identifier related to your name (e.g. initials followed by surname). Some sites with many users avoid name clashes by adding numbers to the user identifier (e.g. Jane Smith is J.Smith1, John Smith is J.Smith2, etc.).

Receiving e-mail

E-mail appears to the recipient as a list of messages from their mailbox presented by an **e-mailer** (software for handling e-mail). The display of the messages is determined by the e-mailer you use. Figures 3.1 and 3.2 show a mailbox displayed by elm (one of several command line UNIX e-mailers) and by PC-Eudora (for Windows).

```
         Mailbox is '/usr/mail/lsap' with 8 messages [ELM 2.3 PL0 (LUT)]

     1    Jul 24 David Riddle       (114)   Review request
  D  2    Jul 25 I Martindale       (15)    Presentations 2
     3    Jul 25 GM Tseng           (17)    July Byte
  N  4    Jul 25 pounderc@hoskyns.c (46)    re: Q from Andrzej Adamski
     5    Jul 25 GF Sargent         (35)    HyperStudio
  N  6    Jul 25 pounderc@hoskyns.c (33)    re: Re: Internet and UK Law
     7    Jul 25 Matthew S. Taylor  (53)    Re: "Old" People
     8    Jul 25 Graham Gerrard     (68)    (Fwd) Earth calling CC (fwd)



        |=pipe, !=shell, ?=help, <n>=set current to n, /=search pattern
  a)lias, C)opy, c)hange folder, d)elete, e)dit, f)orward, g)roup reply, m)ail,
    n)ext, o)ptions, p)rint, q)uit, r)eply, s)ave, t)ag, u)ndelete, or e(x)it
Command: ■
```

Fig. 3.1 *Mailbox displayed by the elm e-mailer*

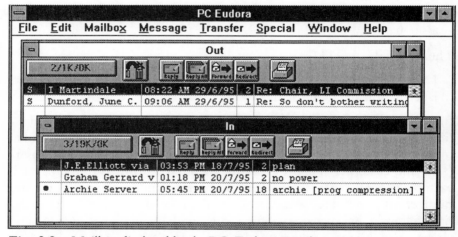

Fig. 3.2 *Mailbox displayed by the PC-Eudora e-mailer*

The elements of a typical e-mail message are shown in Figure 3.3. They include at least:

the sender's name (and/or their e-mail address)
a subject
the date and time sent
the actual message

The **order of messages** is controlled by the e-mailer. The user can usually specify whether messages are ordered by date of arrival, subject, name of sender or message size. All e-mailers allow messages to be read on screen, and printed if necessary. When you read an e-mail message you will

```
Message 3/8   From GM Tseng                    Jul 25 '95 at 11:18 am bst

Return-Path: <G.M.Tseng@lut.ac.uk>
Subject: July Byte
To: A.Poulter
Date: Tue, 25 Jul 95 11:18:58 BST

Alan,

There is lots of good stuff on the Internet in the July Byte.

Gwyneth
```

Fig. 3.3   *The format of a typical e-mail message*

see at the top a **header**. This consists of the sender and recipient's e-mail addresses, the subject, the date and time of sending and routing information. The message itself follows the header. Some e-mailers have primitive facilities for searching for a particular message (e.g. by subject word), or for searching within a message for a word.

All e-mailers allow you to delete messages or to save them in **folders**. A folder is a file of e-mail just like your mailbox, but which you can name in a meaningful way, to enable you to find the e-mail again later. Your e-mailer will allow you to switch to one of these folders to read stored e-mail.

When you exit your e-mailer, it may offer to store all undeleted or unsaved messages in a **received folder**. This will clear your incoming mailbox so that only new messages will appear next time you use it. It is good practice to clear your mailbox each time you use it, although moving it to a received folder can consume an inordinate amount of disk storage space.

See Part III, 'Tips on receiving e-mail' for more detailed information.

Sending e-mail

Sending e-mail involves using your e-mailer to enter the e-mail address of the recipient, a subject (short but descriptive) for the e-mail and last, the actual text of the message. Your e-mailer may store all outgoing messages in an outgoing folder. You can use this folder to review past messages you have sent. It is a good idea, when starting out with e-mail, to practise by sending messages to yourself.

Some people end their e-mail messages with a **signature**, a few lines that say who they are, where they work and give contact information like telephone and fax numbers, as well as their e-mail address. Sometimes signatures contain a witty quote or even a graphic, constructed out of characters on the keyboard. While such personalization is encouraged, overlong signatures (more than four lines) can waste bandwidth. E-mailers can be configured to add a signature to e-mail messages automatically. You may

27

need to create the signature in a separate file first.

Your e-mailer will have a facility to **reply** to a received message. Your reply is usually more meaningful if you add your comments to the text of the original message. You can also **forward** an e-mail message on to another person. E-mail messages that you send, reply to or forward, can be **copied** so that a number of people are sent the same message.

See Part III, 'Tips on sending e-mail' for more detailed information.

Mailing or discussion lists

As well as sending e-mail to individuals, it is also possible to send e-mail to a software program, the most common instance of which is the **mail server**. This is a piece of software which stores a **mailing list** of e-mail addresses of individuals. It can then copy a message from one of those individuals to all the other individuals on the list. Thousands of lists have been set up on the Internet, each devoted to a particular topic, and intended for people who share a common interest to seek, disseminate and share information. In this book we generally use the term **discussion list** which reflects the participative nature of most lists.

Listserv is a widely used mail server program. It originated in the USA and is now used at sites throughout the world by people who have set up discussion lists on their local Internet host computer. In contrast, the **Mailbase** mail server is popular in the UK and runs many discussion lists from a single site (at the University of Newcastle Upon Tyne).

Within librarianship and information science, discussion lists exist which focus on particular professional or research specialisms (e.g. government documents, collection development, information retrieval). Others bring together people who work in a particular type of library (e.g. map, music or law), who use a particular type of system or software (e.g. CD-ROM networks or personal bibliographic software) or who belong to the same professional organization (e.g. the Institute of Information Scientists). Still others have a geographic focus (e.g. library automation in Greece) or are intended for people with a similar job or status (e.g. students, educators).

In the resource guide, the section on 'Discussion lists and electronic conferences' contains a few general-purpose library lists and some useful directories. Of particular note, Stephanie da Silva's *Publicly Accessible Mailing Lists* incorporates hobbyist offerings as well as lists with a more serious purpose. *TILE.NET* provides a complete index of Listserv lists. Diane Kovacs and her team at Kent State University Libraries in the USA produce a multidisciplinary *Directory of Scholarly Electronic Conferences* which contains a section on librarianship. Steve Bonario and Ann Thornton at the University of Houston compile a specialist directory of *Library-Oriented Lists and Electronic Serials* and there is a section devoted to library lists on the *Mailbase Mailing List Service*.

James Milles's *Discussion Lists : Mailing List Manager Commands* provides full instructions for joining and using mailing lists on Listserv, Mailbase and three other popular mail servers (**Majordomo**, **Listproc** and **Mailserv**). This can be requested by e-mail as indicated in the resource guide. Joining a list is usually a simple matter which just involves sending a standard e-mail message to the address of the mail server (mailserver@site-name) leaving the subject line blank. When you join a list you will receive a standard welcome message by e-mail, containing further instructions such as how to contribute messages and to unsubscribe. It is advisable to keep this in a folder for future reference.

In theory, there is no limit to the number of discussion lists you can join. Some discussion lists are **moderated**, which means that there is a person who vets **postings** (messages sent to the discussion list) to ensure their appropriateness, and who may only admit individuals who are truly interested in or knowledgeable about the topic to membership of the list. Since being a moderator involves a lot of work, most discussion lists are unmoderated and these may carry trivial, erroneous or inflammatory postings as well as messages which do fulfil the purposes of the list. Very few discussion lists actually charge for membership.

When you join a discussion list, you will find that postings come with subject lines attached. Replies or further discussion will use the same subject line, usually preceded by '**Re:**', indicating a reply. Replies to your postings may take a while to come in. Generally allow a week. Many messages never generate any replies. When you reply to a posting, include some of the text of the original message. It is not necessary to include all of it, but just enough so that someone who did not see the original posting can follow the debate.

Not all discussion lists allow subscribers to post messages. Some function solely as sources of announcements. We use the term **mailing list** for these, for example *New-list* and *New-lists* which notify subscribers of new Listserv and Mailbase lists respectively.

See Part III, 'Tips on discussion lists' for more detailed information.

Netiquette

Misunderstandings of meaning are possible with e-mail and as a consequence, informal rules of **netiquette**, of how to conduct an e-mail conversation, have evolved. When sending e-mail to an individual, try to make the meaning of the text of your message as clear as possible. E-mail is a form of communication which is much less formal than traditional paper mail, but which does not carry any clues as to emotional undertones, as say, listening to a person's voice in a telephone conversation would. The basic rule is to assume nothing about the recipient (in terms of knowledge, emotional state, or general background) unless you have met them and know them well. Netiquette is even more important when posting to a discussion list, as you have no idea who may be receiving a message.

Some discussion lists have little or no message traffic. Not everyone who is a member of a discussion list posts to the list; members who just read postings sent by other people are known as **lurkers**. There is nothing wrong in being a lurker! Discussion lists, just like any social gathering, are dominated by a few people who do most of the 'talking'. Again there is nothing wrong in this; feel free to join in if you have something to say.

The basic rule for posting to a discussion list is to keep your contribution to the topic of the list. Unmoderated discussion lists, however, are particularly prone to off-topic messages and also to **flames** – messages which are phrased in a heated and sometimes abusive manner. Unless you enjoy public mud-slinging, avoid sending flames and thus getting involved in '**flame wars**'.

See Part III, 'Further netiquette', and 'Discussion list netiquette' for more detailed information.

Disadvantages of e-mail

The classic problem of using e-mail is **overload**. Initially you will get few messages, except from your immediate contacts. Then, as you join discussion lists, your mailbox will start to contain more and more new e-mail each time you look at it. It is impossible to quantify overload. Some individuals despair with more than 10 messages to read; others can deal happily with hundreds. It is important to structure your day to read e-mail efficiently. A session first thing in the morning will tackle e-mail sent the previous afternoon from people in the United States. Another session at the end of the working day will deal with messages sent that day by people closer to home. Be warned that some people deal with overload by never reading or replying to e-mail! Sometimes individuals post advertisements or inane messages to all the discussion lists they can find, whether appropriate or not. This is known as **spamming**. Receiving this sort of e-mail can be extremely annoying.

See Part III, 'Dealing with e-mail overload' for more detailed information.

Another problem of e-mail is its intrinsic lack of **privacy**. Typically, e-mail messages are just text and can be read (albeit with great difficulty) as they are routed from the sender to the recipient via a chain of computers on the Internet. Moreover, the recipient of your e-mail message could forward it on to someone you had not intended. It is never wise to send sensitive information by e-mail. Also e-mail messages can be **faked**. It is prudent to be suspicious about the content of doubtful messages and the identity of senders.

See Part III, 'E-mail privacy, security and anonymity', for more information.

Although e-mail messages are not generally restricted by length, being anything from a word or two to a long discourse, it is difficult to send diagrams or pictures by e-mail. A standard exists, **MIME** (Multipurpose Internet Mail Extension), which your e-mailer may support, for sending all forms of non-textual material via Internet e-mail. However the recipient's e-mailer may not support MIME, so then there is still a problem!

Finally, and perhaps most ironically, another problem of e-mail is not being able to find the e-mail address for a person you want to e-mail! There is no one comprehensive global listing of individual e-mail addresses, basically because such a listing would be enormous, subject to constant flux and difficult to make profitable. E-mail directory services or **White Page Servers** do exist but their coverage is very patchy – even the global **X.500** services. More often than not they do not contain the person you are looking for. It is often easiest to telephone or write to the person you want to e-mail and ask them what their e-mail address is!

See Part III, 'Finding e-mail addresses' for more information.

Advantages of e-mail

So, with these disadvantages, why use e-mail? There are a number of convincing reasons. It can span the globe in minutes. It is free for almost all users, apart from those using certain commercial access providers. Perhaps most important of all is the connection with people that e-mail brings. Questions that cannot be answered by any reference source can be asked on an appropriate discussion list and often bring a flood of responses. While this facility does not work fast enough to be of use at a library reference desk, it is nevertheless impressive. E-mail brings experts from all over the world into your reach. And more than answering the occasional question, membership of a good discussion list brings up-to-the minute news, views, and even gossip on a topic that interests you. There is no substitute in other media for this. Serials, even when produced daily, are behind the times. Radio and television have not got the focus or depth an expert or an aficionado needs. No other media allows the level of interaction with other people that e-mail gives.

Electronic conferencing (USENET)

The second way to communicate with people on the Internet is to use **USENET** (also known as **Netnews**) which is a global **conferencing system**. A conferencing system is similar in purpose to a discussion list, in that each **conference** (or **newsgroup** in USENET terminology) is based on one topic. It differs in that readers of a newsgroup read a common pool of messages which make up that newsgroup, rather than receiving individual copies of each message in their own mailbox.

USENET newsgroups

There are currently around 21,400 newsgroups. Newsgroups are organized into categories, the most important of which are:

Category	*Topic*
bionet	biology
biz	business
comp	anything to do with computers
rec	games, sports and hobbies
misc	topics that don't fit anywhere else
sci	the physical sciences
soc	the culture of countries or social groups
talk	debates on controversial topics
news	topics on USENET itself
alt	'alternative' topics

The precise topic of a newsgroup is indicated by a hierarchical name, which starts with a category e.g:

Newsgroup	*Topic*
comp.mail.elm	the ELM e-mailer
rec.arts.books	novels
sci.maths	mathematics
soc.culture.iran	Iran

TILE.NET provides a complete listing of all USENET newsgroups, including a short description of each one. Newsgroups are also included in the Kovacs *Directory of Scholarly Electronic Conferences*. Like discussion lists, some newsgroups are moderated, which means that postings are screened before appearing. Most newsgroups are not moderated. This can lead to extremely bizarre and/or offensive postings (especially in the 'alt' newsgroups).

Articles and threads

Each newsgroup contains one or more **articles** (messages). Articles in USENET newsgroups look very much like e-mail postings. Like e-mail messages, they all have the name of the person posting them and a subject. Each article has a unique identifying number. Some articles are replies to earlier articles. An article and its replies are collectively known as a **thread**. Articles in the same thread all have the same subject header.

Newsreaders

To access USENET you need a special program called a **newsreader**. Just as with e-mailers, there are a number of different newsreaders, e.g. tin (which has a command line interface) and Free Agent (which is screen-based). Which you use is a matter of availability and personal preference.

All newsreaders operate on three levels. The first level is to display a list of **subscribed to** newsgroups, i.e newsgroups you have chosen to read, together with the number of articles (and possibly threads) they contain (Figures 3.4 and 3.5).

Your newsreader will allow you to move between newsgroups and choose one to read. It will also allow you to see newsgroups that you have not subscribed to and to subscribe to any of them. You will also be able to unsubscribe from (i.e. leave) newsgroups.

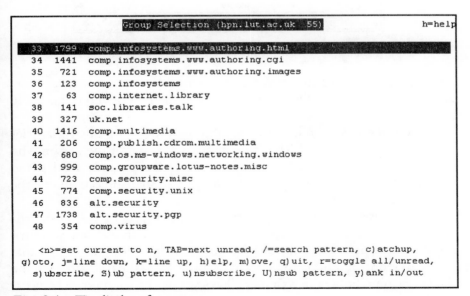

```
                Group Selection (hpn.lut.ac.uk   55)              h=help
  33   1799   comp.infosystems.www.authoring.html
  34   1441   comp.infosystems.www.authoring.cgi
  35    721   comp.infosystems.www.authoring.images
  36    123   comp.infosystems
  37     63   comp.internet.library
  38    141   soc.libraries.talk
  39    327   uk.net
  40   1416   comp.multimedia
  41    206   comp.publish.cdrom.multimedia
  42    680   comp.os.ms-windows.networking.windows
  43    999   comp.groupware.lotus-notes.misc
  44    723   comp.security.misc
  45    774   comp.security.unix
  46    836   alt.security
  47   1738   alt.security.pgp
  48    354   comp.virus

   <n>=set current to n, TAB=next unread, /=search pattern, c)atchup,
g)oto, j=line down, k=line up, h)elp, m)ove, q)uit, r=toggle all/unread,
  s)ubscribe, S)ub pattern, u)nsubscribe, U)nsub pattern, y)ank in/out
```

Fig. 3.4 *Tin display of newsgroups*

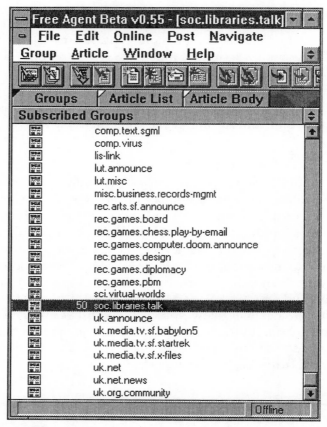

Fig. 3.5 *Free Agent display of newsgroups*

Selecting a newsgroup moves you to the second level of newsreader operation which is to show the articles/threads in the newsgroup (Figures 3.6 and 3.7).

A good newsreader will show only threads and the number of articles they contain. Each thread has a subject and the name of the person who submitted the first article. A poor newsreader will show only articles. You will have to reconstruct threads by looking for similar subjects among the articles. This is a chore.

The last level of newsreader operation is the display of articles/threads themselves. If your newsreader allows you to select a thread, you will then see the first article of the thread. You will be able to read the rest of that article (if it does not fit on the screen) or move on to the next article in the thread. A more limited newsreader allows you to read and move between articles on any subject.

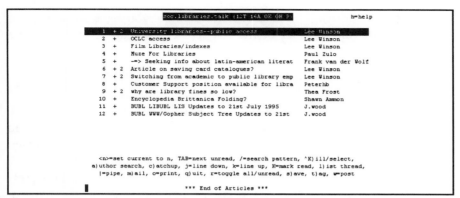

Fig. 3.6   *Tin display of a newsgroup, soc.libraries.talk*

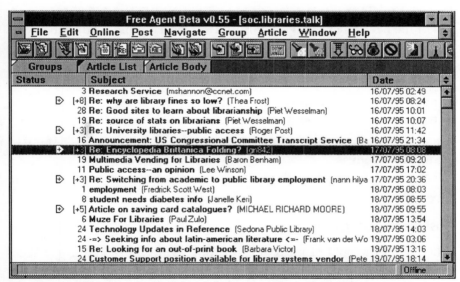

Fig. 3.7   *Free Agent display of a newsgroup, soc.libraries.talk*

Reading USENET

When you have finished reading articles which interest you in a particular newsgroup, it is wise to use your newsreader to **mark as read** all articles in that newsgroup. This clears out the newsgroup and means that next time you read it, only articles posted after your last reading session will be shown. Your newsreader records what you have read in a small data file (usually called **newsrc** or **.newsrc**, depending on your computer's file

35

naming conventions). This lists the newsgroups you have subscribed to and the identifying number of the last article you read in each of those newsgroups.

USENET versus e-mail discussion lists

If this all seems very cumbersome, it is actually easier to read USENET than discussion lists. In your mailbox, messages from different discussion lists are intermixed. Replies to one of your messages may be interspersed throughout your mailbox with messages on other subjects. In contrast, each newsgroup is self-contained. A threaded newsreader can compress many articles into threads and show you on one screen the total activity of a newsgroup. It is possible to read certain discussion lists as USENET groups. These are found in the **bit.listserv** hierarchy. Discussion lists on librarianship topics that can be read as newsgroups can be located via Bonario and Thornton's *Library-Oriented Lists and Electronic Serials*.

For the newcomer though, USENET can be daunting. With e-mail you start with an empty mailbox. With USENET you may start automatically subscribed to hundreds of newsgroups. The best thing to do is to unsubscribe to all groups, except the couple intended for new users:

>   news.announce.newusers
>   news.newusers.questions

When you have mastered reading these, then start looking for more interesting newsgroups.

See Part III, 'Tips on reading USENET newsgroups' for more detailed information.

Posting messages to USENET

Where does the pool of messages that form USENET come from? Your newsreader will enable you to **post** a message to a particular newsgroup. This message is then relayed to neighbouring sites which take their **newsfeed** from your site. These sites will pass on your message and eventually it will reach every site which takes USENET. Incoming messages reach your site in a similar manner, being passed along a chain of newsfeed sites.

Before you post to a newsgroup, be sure you have read the **FAQ** (Frequently-Asked Questions) document, published by many newsgroups. This document is a compendium of the newsgroup's wisdom and is guaranteed to answer obvious questions that might be asked about the topic of the newsgroup. FAQs are normally posted on a regular basis to a newsgroup, at least once a month. For the seeker after information, a FAQ can be invaluable. There is a USENET group which publishes nothing but FAQs, called **news.answers**. *Network News* at the University of Oxford provides a major repository of newsgroup FAQs.

It is also imperative to follow netiquette when posting to newsgroups, just as when posting to discussion lists.

See Part III, 'Tips on posting to USENET newsgroups' for more detailed information.

Access to USENET

Not all sites take USENET and those that do may not take all newsgroups. There are a number of reasons for this. The volume of articles added daily to USENET is immense and requires a lot of central disk storage at a site. As a result articles are **expired** after a set period (which varies between sites) and deleted to save storage space. If you read USENET you must read it regularly or you will miss things! Some newsgroups are intended for an audience within a defined geographical region. Newsgroups in the 'uk' category for example concern UK-related issues and thus are not likely to be taken at a non-UK site. A few newsgroups have to be paid for, notably the 'clari' category which carry copyrighted news stories supplied by Associated Press and Reuters.

Perhaps the main reason why not all newsgroups are taken by many sites is concern over their content. Many newsgroups in the 'alt' category are conduits of all sorts of strange and sometimes unpleasant postings. The 'alt.sex' hierarchy has been widely banned because of worries over its explicit pornographic content. Newsgroups like 'alt.flame' exist only to provoke heated argument. But, just as it is unfair to judge a newsagent's only by its top shelf, USENET contains many stimulating, erudite newsgroups. The advantages of USENET then are very similar to those of e-mail. If the name of a newsgroup does not sound inviting, and a glance at its contents reveals nothing of interest, then move on and look elsewhere.

If your site does not carry USENET at all or does not carry the newsgroup/s you want to read, it is possible to read USENET without a newsreader program. For example, *Zippo Dot Com* allows external users to read articles, but not to post messages.

Interactive systems (IRC, MUDs and MOOs)

Whereas e-mail and USENET are (on the whole) **asynchronous**, in other words, there is normally a time lag between messages being sent and read, some systems allow conversations to be held live and are said to be **synchronous**. Participants have to be simultaneously online but can interact.

One example is **Internet Relay Chat (IRC)** where messages can be typed and received almost simultaneously between users around the world.

Special client software is needed to access IRC. IRC allows you to join a **channel** – a discussion. Channels can be public or private (open to only a few people). Individuals on IRC channels tend to be known by adopted **nicknames**. Using IRC you can list channels, and join and leave channels. Once you have joined a channel, anything you type is echoed to the screens of the other users on that channel, following your nickname. You can list the current individuals on a channel and message them individually if you want.

Conversations on IRC tend to be gossipy. Some sites consider IRC to be nothing but a time-waster and do not allow its use. Occasionally though, IRC can have real importance when news events are reported live by eye witnesses via IRC news channels.

Similar to IRC in that participants are connected in real time, but different in that an imaginary 'locale' is added to contextualize interactions, is a **MUD (Multi-User Dungeon)**. The first MUD was a **role-playing fantasy game** in which participants pretended to be elves, dwarves etc. The MUD would give them a textual description of their character's viewpoint and show them the results of their commands (actions in the MUD). Knowledgeable participants, known as **wizards**, could change or add features to the computer-generated setting. There are now a host of different types of MUD, classified by the capabilities of the software which

```
*** #siam        30      SiamWEB
*** #os/2        36      It's Nightdude's Birthday Party!
*** #bawel       42      bole tulis touic..
*** #teenpics    24      =-=Trade your Gifs & Jpegs Here !! =-= The
+/\/\ad CrE\/\/ =-#1-=
*** #warez~eli 35        MSG an OP except Soccer or pACk1 with one WORKING site
+we don't have for +v & li
*** #pakistan    22      Newpower U S* atleast email once ina while!!!
*** #talk        21      hmmmmm
*** #korea       31
*** #love        41      Don't be a fool don't be blind, heart of mine......
*** #amiga       39      A la carte clue bar to your right, please form a single
+file line
*** #chinese     33      welcome..
*** #WWW         27      Check http://www.yahoo.com/  BEFORE you ask.
*** #unix        32      silence is golden: prove your worth
*** #france      30
*** #windows95 61        for built in winsock or tcp/ip go here -->
+http://www.idirect.com/win95/slp95faq
*** #root        30      Unix, systems, languages, architectures
[1] 15:34 oriole (+i) * type /help for help
```

Fig. 3.8 *An IRC screen*

generates the setting and handles interactions. The latest generation, using up-to-date software techniques, go by the name of **MOO (MUD Object-Oriented)**.

MUDs and their ilk can be extremely enjoyable (if you like role-playing games). However dedicated players have been known to play them to the exclusion of all else. Some sites forbid their use on the same grounds as IRC. MUDs are chiefly textual, but a new generation of graphical MUDs is appearing (for example Worldsaway, from CompuServe). Apart from playing games, MUDs and MOOs can be used for educational purposes (holding tutorials for distant participants) and **live conferencing**. The Kovacs' *Directory of scholarly electronic conferences* now includes MUDs and MOOs that have a scholarly or pedagogical rationale. The *Internet Public Library MOO* was the first, experimental MOO aimed at librarians and library users.

Finally it is possible to **videoconference** via the Internet using the **MBONE (Multicast Backbone)**, an experimental channel running over certain sections of the Internet, down which it is possible to send a continuous stream of packets to more than one site (**multicasting**). Live broadcasts of events have been distributed via the MBONE. Further details can be found on the European *MBONE FAQ*.

Chapter 4
INFORMATION RESOURCES

Information resources – what are they . . . ?

Information resources on the Internet are all stored as **computer files** of some kind. They have a location on at least one Internet site, but may be duplicated at other (**mirror**) sites. Each file has a **filename** (according to the conventions of the computer where it is located) and a **pathname** which defines the **directory** and **subdirectories** in which it is stored, starting from a **root** (initial) directory at its own site (Figure 4.1).

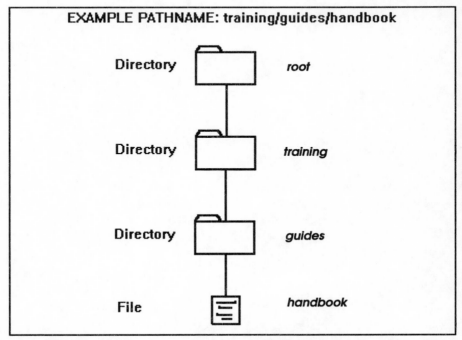

Fig. 4.1   *Schematic illustration of hierarchical file storage*

Typically, a file entitled 'handbook' in the 'guides' subdirectory of the 'training' root directory at a particular site would have a pathname:

training/guides/handbook

Computer files on the Internet contain materials as varied as the text of the King James Bible, images of the Beowulf manuscript, the opening speech from the original Star Trek series, videos of NASA space missions and up-to-the-minute news headlines from CNN.

In this chapter, we identify types of text and software files which are likely to be of interest to the library and information professions generally and then consider how to access the files. Further details of specific resources which are named (in *italics* in the text) can be found in the sections of the resource guide in Part IV which correspond to headings in this chapter.

Directories of Internet resources

Directories of discussion lists, software, library OPACs and other Internet resources are plentiful. The Internet has been criticized for its lack of 'meta-resources' but the situation has changed rapidly over recent years. The real problem is that it is impossible for a single directory to cover its field comprehensively. Moreover, it is not always clear to the user how comprehensive or authoritative a directory is, what precisely it aims to include, or how often it is updated. Too many directories that are not kept up to date can still be found on the Internet. We have included directories of Internet resources in each section of the resource guide, and have aimed to single out ones that complement each other and which are recognized and authoritative.

Discussion lists and electronic conferences – archives and FAQs

Discussion lists and USENET newsgroups only perform distribution, not storage. However, postings to some discussion lists and newsgroups are archived at a site, and these can be helpful to get a flavour for the group before joining. Sometimes they contain compilations of Internet resources pertinent to the subject of the list. In the UK, the *Index of /usenet/* at Imperial College, London provides an archive of USENET newsgroups, while *Deja News* has archives of most mainstream newsgroups going back to early 1995. *Network News* at Oxford University is a good source of newsgroup FAQs. Archives for all Mailbase lists are available via the *Mailbase Mailing List Service*.

Electronic journals, newsletters and alerting services

Electronic serials reflect the diversity that is found in printed publications – from popular magazines, newsletters and newspapers to scholarly academic journals. There are all sorts of hobbyist offerings, fiction magazines and **zines** (small publications usually produced by an individual and not-for-profit) on the Internet, as well as wealth of material aimed at the academic and professional user.

Many electronic journals are freely distributed as text files to members of mailing and discussion lists, though occasionally by USENET. Publication and distribution schedules range from the regular to the highly erratic. Archives of back-issues may be kept at a particular site.

Several publishing companies have announced plans to mount electronic versions of their print-based journals on the Internet. Of course, these will not be free of charge and librarians will need to monitor how prices compare with printed equivalents. Free demonstration versions, which offer contents pages and a selection of articles from well-known serials, are commonplace. Although primarily intended for publicity, these can be useful for alerting purposes.

While electronic journals share many of the characteristics of conventional serial publications, there are differences. Those distributed via e-mail are almost invariably text-only, but some commercial and populist offerings are pioneering the inclusion of graphics. Even text-only e-journals can offer 'value added' features over printed publications. For example, *Public Access Computer Systems Review* enables authors to 'revisit' their articles in order to update them. The 'top' articles, according to how often they are visited in an archive, are monitored.

Scholarly electronic journals have editorial boards and subject articles to peer review which is intrinsically no less rigorous than conventional publishing, so the originally rather guarded response from some sectors of the academic community towards the intellectual authority of scholarly e-journals is disappearing. It is not unusual for academics to take on the roles of e-journal editor, reviewer or distributor on a voluntary basis, thus bypassing the conventional publisher altogether.

The advent of electronic journals has revived the early traditions of academic publishing, whereby readers would enter into a correspondence with the original author. This is easy to do electronically, and in this sense the electronic journal blurs the distinction between a publication and a discussion forum.

In contrast to the scholarly e-journal, the Internet offers a wealth of electronic newsletters which tend to more frequent publication and shorter publication schedules for items of topical interest. *Ariadne* and

Public Access Computer Systems News, for example, are prominent newsletters in the fields of library networking and technology. *Current Cites* is an alerting service which covers a similar field, with citations and short abstracts to articles in other printed and electronic journals.

The *Directory of Electronic Journals, Newsletters and Academic Discussion Lists*, produced by the American Association of Research Libraries (ARL), offers one of the most comprehensive, multidisciplinary listings of e-journals. It is available on the Internet and in print format, and includes a section on library and information studies. Steve Bonario and Ann Thornton's *Library-Oriented Lists and Electronic Serials*, which was mentioned in the last chapter, offers specialist coverage of LIS. Both of these directories can be requested by electronic mail. You can receive notification of new additions to the ARL directory by subscribing to the *NewJour* mailing list. Details are given in the resource guide.

Full text archives

Well-established archives of online books and shorter works available on the Internet include the 'Alex Catalog of Electronic Texts on the Internet', 'Project Gutenberg' and the 'Oxford Text Archive'. These contain the full text of classic works, ranging from translations of ancient Greek and Roman authors to the nineteenth century novel, and covering subjects from politics to religion, history to philosophy. Normally, these are collections of out-of-copyright material which are freely available over the Internet, though still subject to some form of copyright restrictions which prevent redistribution. They are not intended as an alternative to curling up on the sofa with a good book, although the perverse may choose to do so! In fact they are aimed at humanities scholars, for the purposes of content, structural and linguistic analysis and would normally be used in conjunction with indexing, concordance or other text analysis software. As such, they represent a specialized interest, and so we have not included them in the resource guide, though they can be easily traced via information servers such as BUBL.

General reference works

There are some general works of reference to be found on the Internet, notably technical, English and foreign-language dictionaries, thesauri such as Roget's, acronym dictionaries and the like. In the UK, the HUMBUL service at the University of Oxford provides a selection of *Dictionaries and Reference Works*. Some good compilations of reference works from the USA are also included in the resource guide. The commercial reality, however, is that publishers simply do not distribute their material for free. Some encyclopaedia publishers have made their works available for paying users on commercial services like CompuServe and Prodigy; *Britannica Online* offers a free demonstration service.

Networking guides and training materials

There is a plethora of free documents and training materials which are intended for all Internet applications and all types and levels of user. Like selecting a book from a publisher's catalogue, it is not always obvious which to choose so we have picked out a few that give a clear explanation of a range of Internet tools, though there are many more that could be recommended. For example, the *Guide to Network Resource Tools* from EARN/TERENA contains instructions for most of the major network tools. This can be obtained by sending an appropriate e-mail message to the relevant site. The *IETF/TERENA Training Materials Catalogue* is a good place to look for materials to support Internet training courses.

Software

There are many thousands of software packages available on the Internet, both **shareware** (which allows free trial use) and **freeware** for all purposes and all makes of computer. Obviously you will not find mainstream commercial packages. However, documentation for commercial packages can sometimes be found as well as much discussion and information-exchange from user-groups. Networking and general utility software, however, is available in abundance, including a wealth of client and server programs for accessing and setting up Internet applications, and utilities for computer systems support supplied by everyone from enthusiasts to major software companies like Microsoft (on the *EMWAC* server). There are also many specialist applications packages for particular subjects, including librarianship.

Software archives are held at a number of sites on the Internet. For UK users in higher education, *HENSA* is probably the major source while *Shareware.com* acts as a composite site for searching materials in 20 other managed archives. Software can also be located at some of the sites listed in the resource guide under 'Networking organizations', notably the huge, multi-disciplinary *Archive, SunSITE Northern Europe* at Imperial College, London. Although these sites take reasonable precautions, it is always wise to virus check any software you obtain from an archive before running it.

Information resources – how to access them?

Some resources, in the form of files, are delivered automatically by e-mail or USENET. Much, much more is available via the **file transfer protocol** (**FTP**) – a program to connect to a remote site and transfer files there to your own site for reading and use. To use FTP you must know the name of the file you want and where it is located (its site and pathname), but there is a catalogue of files on the Internet (called **Archie**) to help.

FTP was one of the first Internet protocols and although still very widely used, a number of superior methods for setting up and accessing Internet resources have appeared, notably **information servers** (repositories of information) and **gateways** (links to information servers). The first information servers were **bulletin board systems** (**BBS**), followed by **Gopher** and now the **World Wide Web** (known as the **Web**, **WWW** or **W3**). These present users with a series of menus and (in the case of WWW) **hypertext** links which lead to files at the server site or (in the case of Gophers and WWW) to files at any other site on the Internet. The user must have a Gopher or WWW client program to access Gopher or WWW servers. Client and server software for Gopher and WWW is freely available for non-commercial use on a range of computers and details are given in the 'Software' section of the resource guide. If you do not have access to a suitable client, a program called **telnet** can be used to connect to some information servers (indeed, there are some that *only* allow telnet access) but this is primitive in comparison. Many telnet-accessible information servers are offered using a text-based browser program called **Lynx**.

File access using FTP and Archie

Anonymous FTP

Sites use the server version of FTP to make certain files available to anyone. A user needs a client version of FTP. Procedures for using FTP depend on your client, but clients running under graphical interfaces are normally fairly intuitive. Command-based systems are much less so, for example, a typical FTP session running under a UNIX client and server is shown in Figure 4.2. The example shows the retrieval of the latest available edition of Current Cites (an e-journal, path and filename pub/Current.Cites/1995_v.6/1995.6-6) from an FTP site at the University of California, Berkeley.

To start an FTP transfer, you first give the host and domain name of the site to which you want to connect. At the login prompt from the remote site, you enter anonymous. This is the standard response for **anonymous FTP** which allows anyone to log in. Enter your own e-mail address

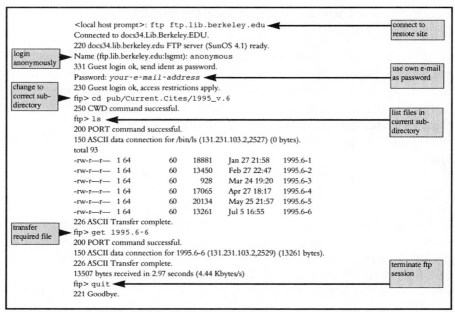

Fig. 4.2 *Example of an FTP session (user's input shown in* this font*)*

at the password prompt which appears next. This is purely a courtesy, so that the operators of an FTP service know who has used it. Finally, you will see a display of a part of the site's file system, containing files for transfer. If you have a graphical FTP client, the procedure is much more intuitive (Figures 4.3–4.8).

Your FTP client will allow remote file/s to be chosen and be transferred to your site. If you find a 'readme' file, transfer and read this first for further information. Your FTP client will also allow you to move around directories at the remote site, but only those for anonymous FTP.

It is good practice to undertake file transfer outside of working hours at the remote site if possible. When you finish you ought to **close**, i.e. terminate the FTP session properly.

You should find the file/s that you transferred in the directory you were using on your computer before you started your FTP client. If you have indirect access to the Internet then you may need to **download** (i.e transfer to your personal computer) the file/s you transferred to your host site using FTP (Figure 4.9).

See Part III, 'Tips on using FTP' for more detailed information.

Fig. 4.3   *Chameleon FTP for Windows, logging in to ftp.lib.berkeley.edu FTP site*

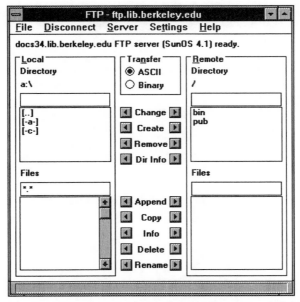

Fig. 4.4   *Chameleon FTP for Windows, viewing the contents of the root directory on ftp.lib.berkeley.edu FTP site*

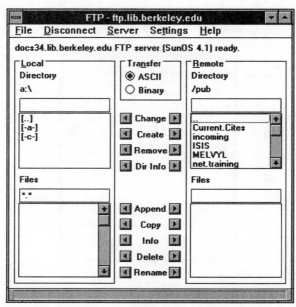

Fig. 4.5 *Chameleon FTP for Windows, viewing the contents of directory pub on ftp.lib.berkeley.edu FTP site*

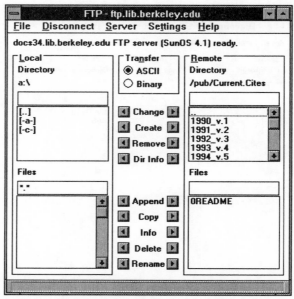

Fig. 4.6 *Chameleon FTP for Windows, viewing the contents of directory pub/Current.Cites on ftp.lib.berkeley.edu FTP site*

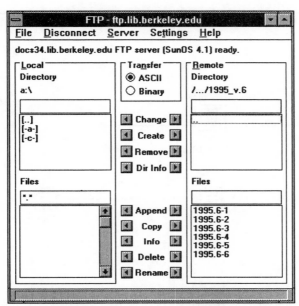

Fig. 4.7 *Chameleon FTP for Windows, viewing the contents of directory pub/Current.Cites/1995_v.6 on ftp.lib.berkeley.edu FTP site*

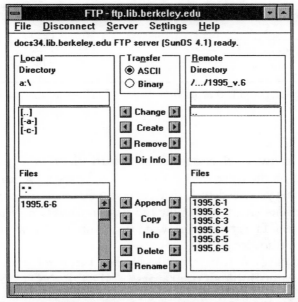

Fig. 4.8 *Chameleon FTP for Windows, having transferred file 1995.6-6 from directory pub/Current.Cites/1995_v.6 on ftp.lib.berkeley.edu FTP site*

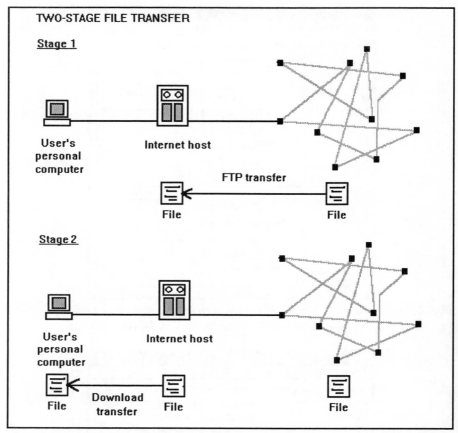

Fig. 4.9 *Two-stage FTP transfer from remote FTP site to personal computer*

Archie

How do you know which site to go to for particular files? A primitive cat-alogue of files on the Internet accessible via an Archie server can help here. To access Archie you need an Archie client or you can connect to an Archie server at a remote site, for example the *Archive, SunSITE Northern Europe* which also lists FTP servers worldwide (listed under 'Networking organi-zations' in the resource guide).

Archie allows you to search for files by their name or part of their name. It does not permit **Boolean operators** (AND, OR, NOT). So, to search for something about BLAISE (an online information retrieval service), you would just enter 'blaise' at your Archie client's search prompt (Figures 4.10 and 4.11). You will get a list of anonymous FTP sites storing files contain-

```
        Welcome to the SUNsite, Department of Computing, Imperial College, UK
             This is the UKUUG supported archie service.

******     This is now archie 3 . 3

This server is really meant for use by UK/European sites. If you are not in this area please try and
find a nearer archie server. Use the servers command to see a full list.

There are a lot of commands, use 'help' for details. Here is a barebones intro:
     set pager              displays output page by page.
     set maxhits N          reset the number of hits returned (default 100).
     set search T           set the search type (default substr).
     prog PATTERN           searches for matches. Eg 'prog bios'.

If you have any problems/queries please email wizards@doc.ic.ac.uk

# Bunyip Information Systems, Inc., 1993, 1994, 1995

# Terminal type set to 'dumb 24 80'.
# 'erase' character is ' ^ ?'.
# 'search' (type string) has the value 'sub'.
archie.doc.ic.ac.uk> prog blaise   ◀▩▩▩▩▩▩▩▩▩▩
# Search type: sub.                              ░░░░░░░░░░░░░░░░░░░░░░
# Your queue position: 1                         ░This search statement is░
# Estimated time for completion: 5 seconds.      ░looking for a file contain-░
working . . . =                                  ░ing the string 'blaise'░
                                                 ░░░░░░░░░░░░░░░░░░░░░░
Host ftp.sunet.se   (130.238.127.3)
Last updated 04:39  13 Jul 1995

     Location: /pub/pictures/views/Croatia
        FILE    -r--r--r--  62351 bytes  01:00  20 Oct 1994  blaise.jpg
Host sunsite.doc.ic.ac.uk  (155.198.1.40)
Lsst updated 04:00  19 Jul 1995

     Location: /recreation/crafts/fido-cfdn/cf-misc
        FILE    -r--rw-r--  1737 bytes  00:00  4 Oct 1994  stblaise.zip

archie.doc.ic.ac.uk> quit
```

Fig. 4.10   *Archie search using a command line client (user's input shown in*
   `this font`)

ing 'blaise' in the title. You then use your FTP client to go to the nearest
site, in geographical terms, and retrieve the file/s you want.

Archie creates its catalogue by automatically indexing files on anonymous FTP sites at regular intervals. Thus it will miss files added since its
last indexing run. Archie can only index files at sites it knows about. Files
can only be searched for by name, so finding information depends on how
adequately a file has been named. Even so, how would you search for a file
containing, say, the text of a paper on the early Industrial Revolution in
Lancashire? There is a crude facility for subject access but this is dependent on file creators adding a description of the file.

Text and non-text files

Computer files fall into two types: text files and non-text (**binary**) files.
Plain text files contain only characters from the **ASCII** character set,

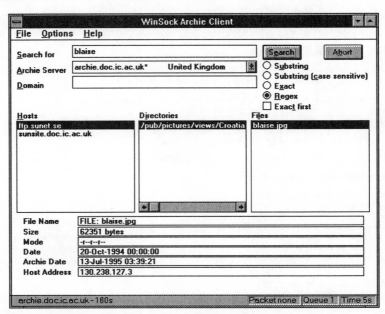

Fig. 4.11 *WSArchie search (graphical client)*

which is used by all computers. Thus they can be stored, displayed and printed on any computer and are reasonably easy to transfer from one computer to another.

Non-text files are always specific to a particular type of computer and possibly operating system as well. To use them in any way almost certainly requires the correct combination of computer and operating system. Transferring non-text files poses more problems than transferring text files.

How do you know whether a file contains just text or not? It is impossible to say from a file name whether the file is a text file or a non-text file. There are **conventions** for filename extensions (i.e the final three characters of the filename) which indicate file format (e.g. 'txt' for text files) but these conventions can be ignored. If you are using a graphical client, the type of file may be indicated by a suitable icon, but really the only definitive test is to transfer a file and then view it with a **text editor**, like EDIT in DOS or Notepad/Write in Windows. If it contains ordinary characters from beginning to end then it is a text file; if it is unreadable or contains unusual characters then it is probably a non-text file. 'Readme' files can be considered to contain text.

You can transfer non-text files using anonymous FTP but you must make your client aware that transfers will be of **binary** (non-text) files, rather than **ASCII** (text) files. FTP clients usually default to ASCII transfers. Choose binary or ascii once you have made the connection to change from one mode to the other. Transferring a file in the wrong mode will render it useless.

File compression

In order to save space on FTP sites, non-text files are usually **compressed** (made smaller by special software which removes repeating elements in a file). Sometimes large text files are compressed, making them into a smaller, non-text file. To use any type of compressed file, once you have transferred it to your computer, you need to **de-compress** it using special software. Unfortunately there are many ways to compress files for each particular type of computer and thus a whole host of programs is needed to de-compress files. The best way to deal with this is to collect as many freeware and shareware de-compression programs for your type of computer as you can. Some forms of compression are used a lot more than others (for example 'zipped' files for PCs).

See Part III, 'File formats' for more detailed information.

Access to sites via telnet (remote login)

The basic means of access to a remote site for anything other than FTP is a **telnet** client. Telnet opens a live link between your computer and an information server or gateway on the Internet, identified by a host and domain name.

How you initiate your telnet client depends on your setup. There may be a suitable icon or, if your host has a command line interface, typically you might enter:

telnet *site-address*   (substituting the actual host and domain
                          name or IP address).

Sometimes a **port number** (e.g. 3000) needs to follow the host/domain name. Once connected, a particular service may require you to **login** using a **public user identifier** and sometimes a password. Often these are shown on the initial 'welcome' screen of the service. The same service may be available at a number of sites; always use the one nearest you, in geographical terms. Try to use a service outside of its normal working hours.

You may be asked to choose a **terminal emulation mode**. This is to allow the remote computer to display text on your computer screen properly. Your telnet client should allow you to choose from a number of terminal emulation modes. The commonest is **VT100**. If in doubt, accept the default offered by the remote system. If the screen looks odd, you have chosen the wrong emulation. Telnet to the site again and choose a different terminal emulation.

Certain information servers and gateways mentioned in the next section can be accessed via telnet.

See Part III, 'Tips on using telnet' for more detailed information.

Information servers and gateways

File access by e-mail, FTP and Archie alone is far too primitive for serious information storage and retrieval. Information servers and gateways provide much easier access to file stores via browsable menu screens, and have been responsible for turning the Internet from a system accessible and usable only by an elite into a global, public, information service. Until the early 1990s, most information servers were run by publicly funded institutions, especially within the higher education and research sectors. Now, droves of public and private organizations of all types are following suit. Many private individuals also set up and maintain servers. The reader is referred to the resource guide section on 'Information servers and gateways' for further details of the examples which are cited below, and to the section on 'Networking organizations' for details of servers offered by some of the organizations mentioned in Chapter 1.

Bulletin boards and Freenets

The earliest form of information server was the **bulletin board** which provided access to information and information services via a series of menus. The software to do this was typically specially written. Bulletin boards usually focus on a particular subject area (e.g. the humanities; library and information studies) or are aimed at certain user groups (e.g. the members of a particular organization). The first bulletin boards gave access to files stored at one site. Many of the chief information servers and gateways in the UK started off as bulletin boards on JANET, such as *The BUBL Information Service* (originally, the **Bulletin Board for Libraries**) and the *NISS Gateway*.

Another early type of bulletin board, intended for **community information**, was the **Freenet**. Freenets are community networks intended to provide free local, cultural, recreational and business information for a particular locality. The first Freenet was in Cleveland, Ohio. They quickly spread throughout North America and there are a few in Europe. In the UK, the public library service at Croydon is investigating community information provision (the *CLIP* project). A Freenet may present a menu that resembles a main street, with choices for the 'town hall', the 'public library' etc. Freenets are accessible from the Internet (e.g. via the *Free-Nets and Community Networks* server), and provide their local communities with limited access to the Internet.

Bulletin boards are usually very easy to use, although it can be tedious going through several menu screens to reach the desired information – especially if what you are looking for is not there after all! There is often no way of anticipating what may be on the next menu screen or of knowing how relevant or complete the information will be when you get to it.

Gopher and Veronica

Gopher was the information server software which really kick-started the growth of the Internet as an information resource. The Gopher software was developed at the University of Minnesota. Internet mythology explains the etymology of the word in that the software literally 'goes for' files at a particular site, a bit like the burrowing animal of the same name (which also happens to be the state symbol for Minnesota).

Gopher clients work by allowing the user to choose an option from a menu (Figures 4.12 and 4.13). This opens either another menu, a file, or a link to some other service. The advantage of Gopher over existing bulletin boards was that these links could be to files on *any* Internet site accessible via FTP, or to *any* service accessible via telnet. The proceedings of USENET newsgroups and discussion lists, if stored as files, could be made available via Gopher. Also links could be made to other Gopher servers run by other sites. What were separate 'islands' of file resources at one site could be made widely accessible by being linked up from one Gopher site to another.

See Part III, 'Tips on using Gopher' for more detailed information.

Gopher clients generally have a **bookmark** facility that allows you to flag a particularly useful menu item or resource so that you can go directly to that item whenever required. Bookmarks can be preserved over time, so that you can easily return to previously discovered Gopher resources.

The success of Gopher in establishing a common standard for information server operation on the Internet led to its widespread use to set up **Campus-Wide Information Systems (CWIS)** at many universities and associated institutions. A CWIS is literally what the name suggests – an information service for a particular academic community. What information it contains depends on the academic community in question. The possibilities are endless: course notes and reading lists for course modules; computing manuals and documentation; the internal telephone and e-mail

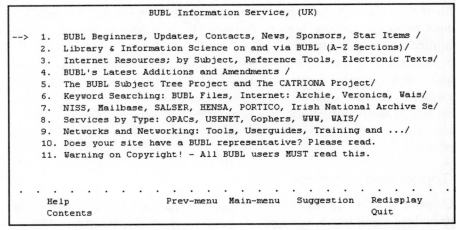

Fig. 4.12 *Opening menu of the old BUBL Gopher using a command line client*

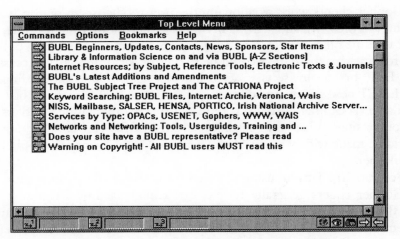

Fig. 4.13 *Opening menu of the old BUBL Gopher using HGopher (graphical client)*

directories; university and course regulations; information from departments, halls of residence, the library, the students' union, student societies and more. Using Gopher means that you can connect from a local CWIS to other campus services (e.g. the library OPAC) and to other Internet Gophers.

Institutions other than universities run Gopher servers. When you start up your Gopher client you may find that you are automatically connected to a local Gopher server run by your own Internet access provider. If not, you can choose a Gopher server by giving your client its address, in terms of host and domain name, and possibly port number. Lists of Gopher servers by country are available, held by nominated **root Gophers**, and these are linked into lists of Gophers worldwide, held on the **Mother Gopher** at the University of Minnesota.

An alternative approach to retrieving information via Gopher is **Veronica**. Veronica is a searchable index of words taken from menu headings on Gopher servers globally. A Veronica search returns a list of Gopher menu titles which fit the search criteria. Most Gopher servers include a link to a local Veronica. **Jughead** is similar to Veronica but only searches for words in menu items on a local Gopher server, or top level menus on a few nominated Gopher servers.

Gopher was a tremendous advance as a tool for retrieving information from a network. However, it has a number of problems. Searching by browsing menus can be tedious. Menu headings may not give a clear idea of what lies beneath them. This is particularly true when the menu leads to another named site on the Internet – you may have simply no idea how useful that site will turn out to be. Gophers are not standardized in that menu items at each level may vary for similar Gophers (e.g. look at any two university Gophers which will contain similar information, but have differently structured menus). The very success of Gopher has meant that when browsing, some choices produce a menu containing hundreds of items. This exacerbates the problem of choosing a browsing path to the information you want. Veronica is excellent, but with no control over terminology in Gopher menu items, searching Veronica is searching an enormous, uncontrolled free-text database. False drops and finding too many or too few menu items are commonplace problems.

World Wide Web

Just as Gopher more or less completely replaced earlier methods of organizing and delivering information over the Internet, so Gopher has been replaced by a newer information server tool, the **World Wide Web**. The World Wide Web began as a **hypertext** publishing project at CERN in Geneva, to create a way of accessing research papers over the Internet. Hypertext is linked text; a highlighted word or phrase in one piece of text, when activated, leads to a different piece of text related to the chosen word or phrase.

Hypertext browsing is not without problems, but it does offer a number of advantages over Gopher's somewhat restrictive menu structures. World Wide Web links can be embedded in text anywhere on a **page**, i.e.

a text file marked up in a language called **HTML (Hypertext Markup Language)**. HTML, a derivative of **SGML (Standard Generalized Markup Language)**, allows the formatting of a page to be controlled by means of **tags**, which indicate the nature of particular page **elements** (title, headings, paragraphs, lists etc). It is possible to embed graphics in pages, making them better looking then text-only Gopher menus (Figure 4.14).

Some World Wide Web clients (for example **Lynx**) can only handle text and thus cannot display graphics (Figure 4.15).

A link to another page or resource is expressed by a **URL (Uniform Resource Locator)**, which gives the retrieval method (usually **http,** the **HyperText Transfer Protocol** for WWW), the host and domain name and the path and file name of the page to be retrieved. For example, the URL for the Internet Resources Newsletter is:

http://www.hw.ac.uk/libWWW/irn/irn/html

where:

http	is the retrieval method
www.hw.ac.uk	is the host and domain name (Heriot-Watt University, UK)
libWWW/irn/irn.html	is the path and filename (the irn.html file in the libWWW/irn directory)

The syntax of URLs is neater than that of Gopher menu links. URLs can be used to retrieve graphics, sound and video. Multimedia links in Gopher are not as simple nor as rich. Finally, URLs can also point to resources under a variety of Internet tools besides WWW (e.g. FTP, telnet, USENET and Gopher) by replacing http in the URL by ftp, telnet, news or gopher respectively. Gopher menu items cannot link to WWW pages.

WWW really took off in early 1993 when the University of Illinois at Urbana-Champaign made freely available for non-commercial use a **WWW browser** (i.e. a WWW client) called **Mosaic** which ran under popular graphical user interfaces like Microsoft Windows, Macintosh and X-Windows. At the time, Gopher clients were predominantly textual. Mosaic became the 'acceptable face of the Internet' and rapidly began to attract commercial interest. The development team of Mosaic left to start their own company, and have produced an even more popular browser, **Netscape**. Mosaic itself attracted commercial licensing deals and many software houses are developing their own WWW browsers. Microsoft has produced a rival to Netscape, *Internet Explorer*.

On startup, all browsers display a user-definable **home page** which

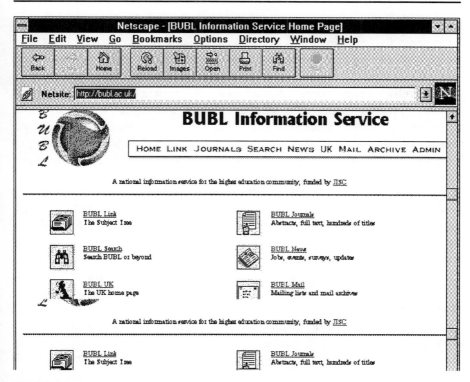

Fig. 4.14 *BUBL WWW server using Netscape*

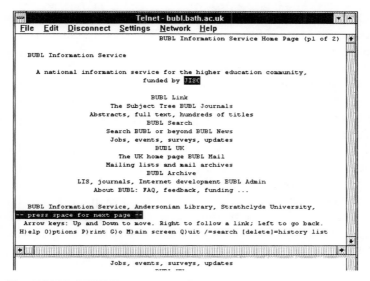

Fig. 4.15 *BUBL WWW server using Lynx*

may be set up by your Internet access provider. You can then click on the links provided, or open a link to any other URL you specify. The links you follow are recorded in a **history list** and there are simple forward and back facilities to retrace your path. All WWW browsers support a **hotlist** facility, whereby you can record the URLs of interesting pages for future reference. Some browsers allow hotlists to be configured hierarchically, to allow the structured storage of URLs for interesting pages. If you do not have a WWW browser, there are publicly accessible browsers available via telnet which present a primitive textual interface to the World Wide Web, notably the *W3 Servers* at CERN.

See Part III, 'Tips for using WWW' for more detailed information.

On the server side, it is easy for people to publish information themselves, as HTML is reasonably straightforward, and software tools for HTML markup are readily available. Creating **personal home pages** got many people interested in publishing information on the Internet.

See Part III, 'Building a WWW page', for more detailed information.

There has been an explosion in recent years of WWW pages and servers listing information on particular subjects. Resources such as electronic journals and networking guides are now becoming available in HTML format giving the advantages of much better presentation, graphics and links to relevant information elsewhere. Just as the University of Minnesota registers international Gopher servers, an international register of *W3 Servers* is held at CERN.

Existing Gopher servers and CWIS have been replaced by WWW. The major UK information servers (*NISS, BUBL,* the *JANET Information Server* etc.) now offer their information via WWW servers. Sites have stopped developing and updating their Gopher servers though they still exist on the Internet as a pitfall for the unwary, who may not realize the information is out of date and no longer maintained.

Like Gopher menus, following links on WWW pages can lead you nowhere. The practice of exploring links to see where they lead, is known as **surfing**. Alternatively, there are equivalents to Veronica, searchable indexes of words in web pages, like **Lycos**, **AltaVista**, **InfoSeek** and **Hotbot**. These massive indexes are created by a software program known as a **spider, robot** or **crawler**, which starts with one WWW page and following all the links it contains, then all the subsequent links and so on. Users' search keywords are matched against the indexes using **relevance ranking** techniques which aim to retrieve and rank the pages which **best match** the user's query and to allocate a numeric score accordingly (how well they do this is sometimes a matter for speculation).

Although these indexes are impressive, the rate of growth at which new WWW servers are appearing makes indexing difficult. There is an ever increasing amount of material to index, and all of it just uncontrolled text. The commercial enthusiasm for the WWW has led to many and varied search tools but none with the universal coverage of Veronica.

Subject listings and indexes

Subject listings

Trying to compile some sort of subject index to Internet resources is a truly Sisyphean task, but one that is being attempted at many Internet sites. At first, some subject guides such as the *Clearinghouse of Subject-Oriented Internet Resource Guides*, were produced as text documents, listing resources under broad subject headings. Nowadays, it is more common to find information servers with resources organized into subject hierarchies. Increasingly specific menu headings lead to lists of resources on particular topics, and URLs or telnet addresses provide a link through to any resource that the user selects.

These are available via services like *BUBL LINK* and *Tradewave Galaxy* and *WWW Virtual Library* at CERN. The biggest of these classified listings, *Yahoo!* from Stanford University, has become a commercial concern.

Some subject listings aim for as wide a coverage as possible across many subjects, for example *BUBL LINK* and *Tradewave Galaxy*. Others such as the *HUMBUL* (humanities), and the Electronic Libraries programme funded 'subject gateways' on the *Access to Networked Resources Projects* offer more selective coverage of quality resources in their fields. All these are aimed at academic and professional users, but others such as *Yahoo!* also include links to resources for leisure and entertainment.

The subject listings services are impressive, but can only be as accurate and comprehensive as the efforts of their compilers allow. This is where services with commercial backing or government sponsorship can score over those maintained by volunteers.

Searchable indexes

An alternative approach to browsing through hierarchical subject menus is to search a keyword index compiled from the text of local files. Some of the subject listings services also offer keyword searching, but this cannot be assumed. At first, there was little standardization in the retrieval features offered by different services, such as methods for truncation, construction of Boolean queries and display of output. In an attempt to rationalize the situation, the **ANSI/NISO Z39.50** standard provides a uniform proce-

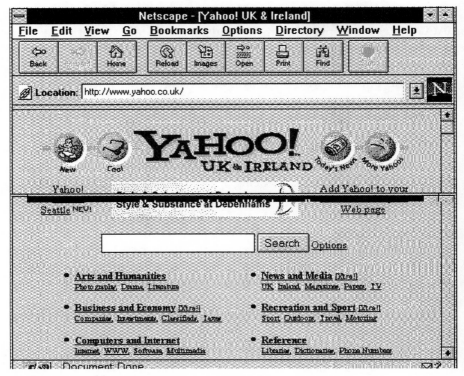

Fig. 4.16 *Yahoo opening screen via Netscape*

dure for client computers to query resources at server sites, based on a single user-interface. Z39.50 is rapidly gaining wide acceptance.

WAIS

WAIS (Wide Area Information Server) is a particular type of searchable index. It was the first database server to support the Z39.50 protocol and it provides keyword searching across WAIS databases and relevance ranking of found items. There are several hundred WAIS databases, many of which contain texts of Internet help or the past proceedings of discussion lists or USENET newsgroups. WAIS servers are sometimes provided at a site to search the files at that site, not across the 'whole Internet' as the aforementioned searchable indexes attempt to do. However, one or more WAIS databases can be searched at once using a WAIS client. If you do not have a WAIS client, WAIS can be accessed by telnet, Gopher and WWW on several of the services already mentioned.

OPACs and library-based information servers

The **online public access catalogues** (OPACs) of about 70 academic and research libraries in the UK – and thousands more in other parts of the world – can be accessed via telnet, Gopher and the WWW. *Hytelnet* provides authoritative listings of what is available throughout the world while the *CARL Network of Libraries and Databases* links to hundreds of public, academic and school libraries in the USA. The *UK Higher Education Library Catalogues* from NISS is the major gateway to UK OPACs.

Unfortunately, if you want to trace bibliographic details of a hard-to-find item, there is no easy way of knowing which OPAC to try, although NISS does attempt to indicate subject strengths of particular OPACs. Coverage of this information is, however, patchy.

There are many software platforms for OPACs offered by different commercial library automation suppliers. They each have their own search procedures. Although on-screen help is invariably provided, and basic instructions for searching most of the major systems are available through directories like *Hytelnet*, this situation is far from ideal. Hence many of the first applications of Z39.50 were initiated by libraries in the USA to provide an alternative but standard method for searching their bibliographic holdings data and other databases such as circulation files. So far, few UK libraries have followed suit, though some library system suppliers are just beginning to offer an option for access via Z39.50 servers.

In many respects though, library automation systems are lagging behind the facilities offered by free WWW software. Traditional OPACs look drab compared to WWW and to counter this, some libraries are putting experimental WWW front-ends over their OPACs. Like library-based Gopher servers before them, the best of these give access to a wide range of library services in addition to the OPAC itself. User education programmes, point-and-click library tours, special exhibitions, library promotional materials and much, much more can be offered. Using a suitable **forms-based browser** (such as Explorer or Netscape), forms can be set up for users to enter book and interlibrary loan requests or OPAC searches. Even more ambitious, a number of digital library projects have started to investigate the many technical, legal and commercial issues at stake in providing full text search and display of electronic documents. A good example is the 'Initiatives for Access' project from the British Library, details of which are available on their *Portico* server, and of course the *Electronic Libraries Programme* which was mentioned in Chapter 1.

Academic libraries in the USA have been particularly active in setting up WWW servers to interface to their resources and services. Eric Lease Morgan provides a good selection of *Online Catalogs with Webbed Interfaces* while Ken Middleton's *Innovative Internet Applications in Libraries* is a good place to start investigating the imaginative range of different services which (mostly) US libraries are now offering over the Internet. Thomas Dowling's *Libweb* links to library-based WWW servers world wide, including a number in Europe and the UK. There is a discussion list, *Web4Lib*, for librarians who are interested in setting up library-based Web servers and clients.

In addition, some major national catalogues and bibliographies are available – the Library of Congress catalogue (Locis) is searchable via the *Library of Congress Home Page* (including a Z39.50 facility if you have a Z39.50 client). The British Library's prototype network OPAC is available at over 200 JANET sites, and WWW access is being piloted at one or two test sites.

Information servers from other organizations

The advent of the WWW has seen a burgeoning number of information servers being set up by organizations of all types, often to promote the

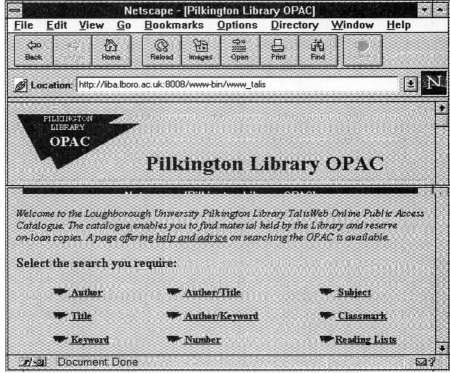

Fig. 4.17 *Loughborough University WWW OPAC via Netscape*

organization and its goods and services. The last sections of the resource guide are devoted to organizational servers that will be of general interest to library and information professionals. Of particular note here, catalogues from over 40 UK publishers are now available, and a rapidly growing number of bookshops are offering booklists and online ordering to the public at large. Broadcast and news media are offering TV and radio schedules, news summaries and the like. Further information can be found in the resource guide under 'Booksellers, publishers and the media'.

Many of the commercial online information retrieval services are accessible by telnet, bringing free if not necessarily more reliable telecommunications links to these services for many subscribers. Hence we have broken our rule of listing only free resources, and devoted a section of the resource guide to 'Commercial online information retrieval services'. A few online retrieval services have set up public information servers providing system and database documentation, plus links to the search service for subscribers.

Also spotlighted in the resource guide are 'Government, government-related and international organizations', 'Library and information education', and 'LIS and related professional associations'.

Cataloguing of Internet resources

There is no single definitive catalogue or index to the Internet and given its size it would be impractical to try to build one. Some machine generated indexes can already provide access to millions of items but such huge centralized indexes must eventually suffer from degraded performance problems. Libraries are selective in their choice of materials, carefully matching their collections to meet user needs. Similar careful selection process are required when it comes to cataloguing Internet resources.

There are a number of projects currently looking at the area of cataloguing and the Internet, each taking slightly different approaches to the problem. The **OCLC Internet Cataloging Project** is looking at extending the model of the traditional library catalogue. This involves a group of volunteer libraries creating catalogue records for networked resources. The records conform to US MARC standards and will be integrated within local and national library catalogues such as the 'OCLC Online Union Catalog' and the 'First Search' database. A similar project in the UK is **CATRIONA** (CATaloguing and Retrieval of Information Over Networks). This project proposes to use UKMARC to create local catalogue records of networked resources. CATRIONA also proposes to enhance a range of standard OPAC clients to provide distributed searching and the ability to retrieve resources across the networks.

A different approach is the use of specially designed templates for describing resources. The **IAFA** (Internet Anonymous FTP Archive) group of the IETF (Internet Engineering Task Force) have produced a series of templates that are now being used by a number of services and projects, including **ALIWEB** and the **ROADS** project in the UK. A similar approach has also been taken by *NISS* who have developed a template to describe resources on their subject gateway.

A third approach is to produce descriptive information in the headers of network documents. The **Text Encoding Initiative (TEI)** is an international project to provide guidelines on encoding and interchanging machine-readable texts in the humanities. The header provides bibliographic information and a description of the document, that would be created at source by its author or publisher. This sort of **metadata** has also been proposed for use in HTML documents. References to all these projects can be found in the resource guide entry *Digital Libraries: Cataloguing and Indexing of Electronic Resources*, listed under 'OPACs and library-based information servers'.

PART III
Using the Internet effectively

Contents

INTRODUCTION TO PART III

This part contains advice on how to use the Internet effectively. It assumes that Part II has been read or that the reader has a basic knowledge of Internet resources and tools. Unless otherwise noted, resources mentioned in this part appear under 'Utilities' in Part IV, the resource guide.

Chapter 5
E-MAIL AND USENET

Tips on receiving e-mail

E-mail tends to accumulate quickly over time. If you have e-mail only, or indirect access to the Internet, you may find that you exceed your **disk quota** (permitted storage space) on the computer that stores your e-mail. **Mail-bombing** is the unpleasant practice of deliberately sending someone a large amount of e-mail so that their disk quota is exceeded.

It is advisable to delete most of the e-mail you receive, unless you really think you will need to refer to it later. Another way of saving on storage space is to disable (using your e-mailer) your outgoing and received folders. If you want to retain any messages, store them in folders that you name yourself (your e-mailer should allow you to do this). E-mail in suitably named folders is easier to find later, for reference or deletion. Of course, you can always print your e-mail, and then delete it.

If you have e-mail only, or indirect access to the Internet, it ought to be possible to **download** e-mail from your Internet host onto your personal computer. This will enable you to store e-mail locally and delete it from the host computer. This is, however, inconvenient if you need to redistribute a copy of a downloaded e-mail message, as you must **upload** it back onto your host computer first. You will need to check with your Internet access provider about appropriate software for downloading and uploading.

Some e-mailers, such as Eudora, are known as **off-line readers**. They automatically download e-mail from your host computer to your personal computer in order to avoid online connection charges while reading e-mail.

If you have a direct Internet connection, your e-mail will automatically be stored on your own computer.

Tips on sending e-mail

Composing messages

If you have e-mail only, or indirect access to the Internet, you do not have to use the editor supplied on the host computer to compose messages if it does not suit you. Instead you can prepare your e-mail messages using a word processor on your personal computer and then transfer (**upload**) them to your host system using appropriate communications software. You will have to save each e-mail message composed with your word processor as a text file so that they can be uploaded. All word processors can save to a text (ASCII) file.

If you have direct access to the Internet, your e-mailer ought to contain a reasonably user-friendly editor. If not, then try 'copy and paste' under a graphical user-interface, to transfer text into your e-mailer. It is also possible to send e-mail with a **mail-enabled** word processor. This involves use of the 'print' command to e-mail the current document instead of printing it. You will need to consult your Internet access provider about whether this is possible.

Storing addresses

To avoid having to type e-mail addresses for regular correspondents over and over again, your e-mailer should allow you to set up **aliases** (also known as **nicknames**) which link short names (e.g. Jane) with full e-mail addresses (e.g. J.X.Smith@bl.uk). You only have to enter the short name when addressing e-mail. Your **alias list** functions like an address book for e-mail identifiers. If someone e-mails you first, your e-mailer ought to be able to create an alias from the address details in their message.

Confirming receipt

When you have sent an e-mail to someone, how do you know whether it has been received and read? You know that it is in the addressee's incoming mailbox if the message does not **bounce** (i.e. return to you because of some error, typically an incorrect address). Bounced e-mails will contain a reason for their return.

Unfortunately, it is impossible to know if the e-mail has been read. The best you can do is know if the recipient has logged in after you sent the e-mail. There is a piece of software called **finger**, which takes an e-mail address and tells you when that person last logged in. Note that not all sites allow their users to be 'fingered' from remote sites, as this is seen as a security risk.

If you are worried about the receipt of an urgent e-mail, you can try e-mailing the **postmaster** at a site. The postmaster is the person responsible for managing the e-mail system at a site and all sites should have one. The postmaster's e-mail address is always postmaster@*site*.

Finding e-mail addresses

It is usually straightforward to find the e-mail address of someone at your own site. Ask your Internet access provider about local directory services (**WHOIS** is often used). It can be a bigger problem to find an address for someone at a different site. You are advised to consult the list of services on the *White Pages*.

Further netiquette

To the basic rules of netiquette one can add many more, which are appropriate in different circumstances. Arlene Rinaldi's *The Net: User Guidelines and Netiquette* is a well-respected guide. Perhaps the only significant point to add to her recommendations is to avoid using culturally specific language. UK colloquialisms or metaphors may not be understood abroad.

All e-mail messages (and USENET postings) have to be formed from the characters on a keyboard. To reduce the time spent keying text, a range of **abbreviations** and **jargon terms** are in common usage. **Newbie**, for example, is a person new and inexperienced in Internet lore. Many abbreviations can be deduced from their context, e.g. **btw** for 'by the way', **IMO** for 'in my opinion'. The *Jargon File Resources* is an extensive glossary of such abbreviations.

Finally, to try to add a measure of emotional undertone to text messages, **smileys** (also known as **emoticons**) have evolved. Created from keyboard characters, they are to be imagined as a face laid sideways, e.g.

> **:-)** is a smiling face (indicating humour);
> **:-(** is a sad face (indicating regret).

There is an *Unofficial Smiley Dictionary* in the EFF's 'Big Dummy's Guide to the Internet'.

E-mail privacy, security and anonymity

If you are worried about privacy or security (e.g. sending sensitive information by e-mail) then use standard **encryption**. Encryption software works by encrypting (transforming) your text into a near-random string of characters, using a **password**. This password is required to get the encryption software to change the encrypted message back into text. Some e-mailers offer encryption facilities.

There are two problems with using built-in e-mailer encryption. Firstly, the recipient must be using the same e-mailer. Secondly, and even more crucially, you must somehow send the password to the recipient. Sending the password in an ordinary e-mail defeats the purpose of using encryption in the first place.

Public/private key encryption gets around this problem. Encryption is linked to two machine-readable keys: a public key, which can be sent by ordinary e-mail and a private key, which is kept on a local computer. To communicate, both parties exchange public keys by ordinary e-mail. The sender then encrypts a text message using their private key and the public key of the recipient. This encrypted message is then sent to the recipient by e-mail. To decrypt this message the recipient needs their private key and the public key of the sender. This process not only removes the need for sending a password but also means that, using keys, each party can verify that the other party was the sender/recipient.

A freeware program, **Pretty Good Privacy** (PGP) has become the *de facto* Internet standard for this means of communication. Other uses of public/private key encryption relate to the authentication of messages by appending machine-readable **digital signatures**.

There are two problems. Firstly, you need to trust that an individual's public key really does belong to that person. Secondly, public/private key encryption is viewed askance by some government security agencies as it can defeat their attempts to decrypt messages. This has lead to restrictions on its use. It is currently illegal to export PGP from the United States, although PGP is freely available world wide. There are no current restrictions on its use in the UK. *Cryptography, PGP and Your Privacy* explains how to obtain and use PGP.

As well as hiding the content of a message, there may also be a need to hide the identity of the sender. Anonymous e-mail is rightly frowned on in some quarters, but it has legitimate uses. For example, it is vital to the Samaritans who now can be contacted by e-mail and need to preserve the anonymity of their callers.

Anonymous e-mail is achieved using a **remailer**, a computer at an intermediate site which accepts an e-mail with a normal identifier which it strips off before forwarding the e-mail to its intended destination. See the *Anonymous Remailers* FAQ for more information.

Tips on discussion lists

Using the correct address

It is important to distinguish between a mail server address (to which you send subscription requests) and the address of the discussion list itself (to which you send your postings). For example, to subscribe to PACS-L (which uses the Listserv mail server) you would send e-mail to:

listserv@uhupvm1.uh.edu

whereas you would send postings to:

pacs-l@uhupvm1.uh.edu

Do not send subscription requests to the discussion list address. When you follow discussion lists, you will see the occasional subscription message incorrectly posted by would-be subscribers.

If you are responding to a posting on a discussion list, ask yourself whether it is really appropriate to reply to all the participants or just to the original sender. Before you dispatch your reply, check whether your e-mailer is sending it to the discussion list or to the person who posted the message. Some personal replies to postings are inadvertently sent to the entire membership of a discussion list.

List owners

A mail server does not run unattended. A **list owner** is a person who oversees the operation of a particular mail server, usually pertaining to the running of a specific discussion list on that mail server. The list owner will, for example, notify subscribers if postings to a discussion list are lost. A list owner's function is not the same as a moderator of a discussion list, although the two functions can be handled by the same person. The e-mail address of the list owner is usually included in the subscription details for a discussion list.

Discussion list netiquette

Before posting a question to a discussion list, make sure that the answer is not already available as a FAQ. You can ask for responses to your questions to be sent to you personally. Remember to give your e-mail address. Thank any respondents and distribute a brief summary of your answers via the discussion list. The best way to get questions answered is to be known, for example by having replied to other people before. When asking a question, always say how you have tried to find the answer yourself.

If an inflammatory or totally off-topic posting is made to a discussion list you follow, wait at least 24 hours before complaining about it. Other subscribers will probably express the same concerns as you. For a flagrant breach of netiquette (for example an off-topic unsolicited advertisement), you can complain to the list owner of an unmoderated list or, more seriously, to the postmaster at the site where the offending message was posted. If you inadvertently make an off-topic posting to a discussion list, a swift apology should settle things.

Additional features of mail servers

Mail server software can do more than just handle subscription requests. For a complete list of commands which can be given to a particular mail server, send it an e-mail message consisting of the word help.

If an **archive** of previous postings is kept, it may be searchable by commands sent to the mail server. Sometimes associated files for a discussion list (for example a FAQ) can be retrieved via a mail server command. The membership of a discussion list can also be retrieved by e-mail. This is sometimes useful to discover the e-mail address of a particular contributor whom you wish to contact personally.

Dealing with e-mail overload

E-mail can quickly accumulate over holiday periods and at other times when you are unable to read it. While there is nothing you can do about personal messages, e-mail from discussion lists can be temporarily halted. To do this, you need to send a special command to the mail server addresses of each discussion list to which you subscribe, and similarly to resume receiving messages again. Appropriate commands for different mail servers are given in James Milles's *Discussion Lists: Mailing List Manager Commands* which appears under 'Discussion lists and electronic conferences' in the resource guide.

Some discussion lists, if they are particularly busy, offer subscribers a **digest** option which, if chosen, means that you get all the postings made over a time period (typically a day) batched, indexed and sent to you in a single e-mail. While this reduces the number of e-mail messages you receive, digest e-mails can be very large and slow to skim through to get to the postings that interest you.

The main problem with incoming e-mail is that it is usually sorted in order of arrival. This mixes up e-mail from different discussion lists with personal e-mail. A **mail filter** or a **rules-based e-mailer** is software which automatically saves incoming mail to different folders according to rules (instructions) that you define. For example, e-mail from discussion lists can be stored in separate folders, one for each list. This leaves only personal e-mail in your incoming mailbox. If you are short of time, you can just deal with your personal e-mail. The only disadvantage is that you may forget to read and delete e-mail from the other folders. This may cause storage space problems.

A primitive alternative is to acquire more than one e-mail address, for example one for personal e-mail, the other for discussion list e-mail. Ask your Internet access provider if this is permitted.

It is also possible to read certain discussion lists as USENET newsgroups. A good newsreader offering threading is vastly superior to a standard e-mailer. Some discussion lists are widely available in the **bit.listserv.** hierarchy. Check this first for the discussion list you want. Each newsgroup beginning bit.listserv. ends with the name of the discussion list it covers (e.g. bit.listserv.pacs-l for the PACS-L discussion list).

You can ask your Internet access provider to create a newsgroup for the e-mail messages from a discussion list. If a number of people at your site want to read the same discussion list, this economizes on disk space because the messages only need to be stored once at your site (rather than copies in each subscriber's incoming mailbox).

Tips on reading USENET newsgroups

Be very selective in choosing which newsgroups to read, and wary about subscribing to newly created newsgroups. You may still find that you cannot read all the newsgroups that you would like. In this case you must order the newsgroups (your newsreader will have a command for this) so that they are displayed to you in priority order. You can then simply work your way down them until you run out of time or inclination.

Deciding which newsgroups to read

Whatever your personal choice of newsgroups, there are a number which are worth considering generally. There are currently only two library/information oriented newsgroups, **soc.libraries.talk** and **comp.internet.library**.

Your Internet access provider or site may provide local newsgroups. If these relate to local user support then they are well worth following.

The **uk.** hierarchy of newsgroups is growing fast. The newsgroup **uk.net.news** is where new newsgroups are discussed and announced.

There are a large number of newsgroups whose names end in '.announce' which cover announcements in a particular area. They are worthwhile because there is no chatter, just a few articles on new Internet resources or information. Your newsreader should allow you to search all newsgroups (not just the ones you subscribe to) for the word 'announce' to find those newsgroups.

Finally, if you find a particularly relevant article in one newsgroup, look to see if it has been **crossposted** (that is posted to a number of newsgroups at once). These other newsgroups might also be of interest to you.

Reading articles and threads

Only read threads that look interesting to you. You do not have to read every article in every thread. Get to recognize who posts articles you find most relevant. Read the initial articles in the longest threads (as these are obviously of interest to the newsgroup audience). Remember to mark all articles as read before you leave the newsgroup, so that next time you will see only new articles.

A facility offered by most newsreaders is the **kill file**. A kill file is a stoplist of subject words or individuals' names which, if attached to an article, prevent that article from appearing in your newsreader. The problem here is to know what to reject.

There are generally two ways of saving interesting articles or threads from your newsreader. The first involves saving them as a file on the computer you use to read USENET. There ought to be a command for **tagging** several articles to save them collectively. The second method sends an article, or a thread, or a set of tagged articles to your e-mail address. You can then deal with the article(s) as e-mail.

Tips on posting to USENET newsgroups

The basic rule is to follow netiquette. Comments made before about posting to discussion lists also apply to posting to newsgroups.

Posting via a newsreader can be tricky. You will need to know the name of the newsgroup (or names if crossposting). You may need to give a geographical distribution for your message (usually a choice of site, uk or world). You may also be requested to add keywords, but these have little relevance in practice.

If you have an indirect Internet connection, then your newsreader may call up an editor for you to enter your article. It may be possible to change this editor if it is not to your taste; consult your Internet access provider about this. Finally, before you post, check whether your newsreader will append your signature file.

There is a newsgroup called **misc.test**, which you can use to practise posting. Use it until you are confident of the posting procedure employed by your newsreader. Your newsreader ought to let you reply to other people's articles. Replies are easier than posting new articles.

Perhaps the easiest way to post to USENET is to use the *Deja News Post Newsgroup Article* service. Articles can be submitted directly by registered users or via an e-mail confirmation by unregistered users.

Chapter 6
USING AND CREATING RESOURCES

Accessing Internet resources by e-mail

Do not despair if you only have e-mail access to the Internet. You can still use (albeit slowly) all the tools for finding and retrieving files, like FTP, Archie, Gopher and WWW. Bob Rankin's *Accessing the Internet by E-Mail*, available by e-mail request, is the definitive guide.

Tips on using FTP

There are a few things to remember whatever type of client you are using for FTP. The first is to check the size of a file before transferring it. The bigger the file, the longer it will take to transfer. Try transferring a small file first to get an idea of how long bigger files will take. Second, if you find one useful file on an FTP site, there may be more. Look for a file named 'readme', 'index', 'contents' or something similar. This ought to contain a description of all the files in the current directory on the remote site. Sometimes it is worth browsing directory trees on FTP sites, looking for interesting files.

To read a text file, you normally transfer it to your own site first, then use a local editor or word processor. It is, however, possible to read a text file while still connected to a remote FTP site. The way to do this is dependent on your level of access, FTP client and computer system, so you must consult your Internet access provider for details.

Some FTP sites are very busy and difficult to access, particularly those which offer special collections of files. For example, the *EMWAC* archive contains applications software for Microsoft Windows. Busy sites are sometimes replicated at **mirror sites** elsewhere in order to spread the load between them. The *Archive, SunSITE Northern Europe* is the main mirror site in the UK. It mirrors a number of the largest FTP sites in the USA. Further details appear under 'Networking organizations' in the resource guide.

FTP can also be used to transfer files to, rather than from, a remote site. This is known as **uploading**. For security reasons many sites do not allow this. Those sites that do usually have a directory called **incoming** to receive files. Uploaded files should be at least accompanied by a description of their contents and the uploader's name and e-mail address. If considered suitable for the collection at the remote FTP site, uploaded files will be transferred to an appropriate directory. If not, they will almost certainly be deleted.

Finally, it is possible to be registered for special access rights at an FTP site (for example, if you have useful files to upload to it) and for this you will be given a user identifier and password which you should use instead of logging in anonymously.

Using a command line FTP client

There are a number of extra complications involved in using a command line FTP client. The commands that are used depend on your client program and on the operating system at the remote site. Many FTP sites still use UNIX machines, and the basic procedures for using these are shown in Table 6.1. Commands typed by the user are shown in `this font`.

You will probably find it difficult to distinguish files from directories in listings from the remote site (usually obtained by the command `ls`). Directories are indicated by a 'd' at the beginning of the line. If you try to transfer a directory by mistake, you will get an error message. Changing to a directory (usually done by the command `cd`) may require that you enter its name *exactly* (character for character and case for case) as it appears in the listing. Finally, when transferring a remote file (usually with the command `get`), an error will occur if the name of the remote file does not conform to the file-naming conventions of the computer running your FTP client. The solution is to give the file name on the remote system first (usually character for character, case for case), and then a new file name acceptable to your computer system.

File formats

There is a multiplicity of **file formats** for non-text (**binary**) files. Many of these relate to graphics, sound and video, and are recognizable by the characters following the final full stop in a file name. Some file-naming conventions are common to several types of computer; others specific to PC compatibles, Macintosh machines etc. Examples of **graphics types** are **.gif**, **.jpg**, and **.bmp**.

79

Table 6.1 Basic commands for anonymous FTP using a command line client

(Substitute actual information for items shown in *italics.*)

Connecting and disconnecting to a remote FTP site

ftp *site-address*	Type this at your system prompt to connect to a remote site.
Name: anonymous	At the prompt from the remote site, request anonymous login.
Password: *your e-mail-address*	Use your own e-mail address as a password (it will not appear on screen as you type it).
quit	Close FTP session and return to local host.

Moving around directories and transferring files

ls	Display the contents of the current directory (short format).
ls -l dir	Display the contents of the current directory (long format).
cd *directory-name*	Change to the immediately subordinate or the immediately preceding directory.
cd *directory-path*	Change to a subdirectory specified by the directory path.
cd/	Return to the root (login) directory.
binary	Change to binary transfer mode (before transferring a binary file).
ascii	Change to ASCII (text) transfer mode.
get *filename*	Transfer the specified file from the current directory on the remote host to the current directory on your local host.
mget *filenames*	Transfer several files from the current directory on the remote host to the current directory on your local host. Remote filenames should be separated by a space and can include wildcards (* or ?) in the filename.
?	Request help.

Most binary (and some text) files have been compressed. These must usually be de-compressed before they can be used. Then a further piece of software (e.g. a **graphics file viewer** for graphics files) might be needed. The *Multimedia File Formats on the Internet* is an invaluable help in sorting out what needs doing to make a downloaded file useable. It recommends a number of software packages for de-compression and the like which can then be found in the software archives listed under 'Software' in the resource guide.

To be on the safe side, all software should be checked for viruses before running it. Excellent **virus checkers** are also available from software archives.

Tips on using telnet

If you have a command line telnet client, then you will need to be familiar with a few basic telnet commands. Telnet commands can vary because of differences in operating systems and the way that telnet is implemented at different sites. However, the procedures given in Table 6.2 should work on most systems.

Table 6.2   Basic procedures for using a command line telnet client
(Substitute actual information for items shown in *italics*.)

Connecting and disconnecting to a remote site (Remote telnet)	
telnet *site-address*	Type this at your system prompt to connect to a remote site. Use the actual host and domain name, or the IP address.
login: *userid*	At the login: prompt from the remote site, respond with the public user identifer. (Some sites may also require a password).
terminal type: vt100	Try vt100 if you are asked for a terminal type, or accept any default offered by the remote site.
^]	(Control and right bracket keys) Escape sequence to interrupt connection and return to local telnet client.
^- ^c ^d ^}	Alternative escape sequences which are sometimes used.
Local telnet	
telnet	Initiate local telnet.
quit	Exit from telnet.
close	Close current connection.
?	Display other local telnet commands.

Once connected to a remote site (**remote telnet**) then you will need to be familiar with the procedures at that site, or follow the on-screen instructions which are provided by most public-access telnet services. The procedures for disconnecting again vary considerably from site to site. Sometimes instructions are given on the opening screen only, so always make a note of this. This is also true of the **escape sequence** to interrupt the connection in an emergency. Using the escape sequence returns you to **local telnet** (the telnet program on your machine), indicated by the prompt:

telnet>

You can then use the `quit` or `close` command to disconnect properly.

Tips on using Gopher

If using a command line Gopher client, or a telnet connection to a Gopher, then the commands available at any point are always summarized at the bottom of the screen (Figure 6.1). Always take note of these.

Note that menu items may not all fit on one screen. A 'page x of y' message will indicate how many more screens full of items follow the one you are looking at. It is a common mistake to ignore continuation menu screens. Menus entitled 'All the Gopher servers in the world' are extremely lengthy, and best avoided if you can find a suitable alternative.

The basic commands for navigating menus are summarized in Table 6.3. In addition, after you have displayed a text file, you may be given the option to e-mail it to yourself, or to save or download a file to the computer which is running your Gopher client. These commands are not available on all servers, and you cannot save or download if you made a telnet connection to the server.

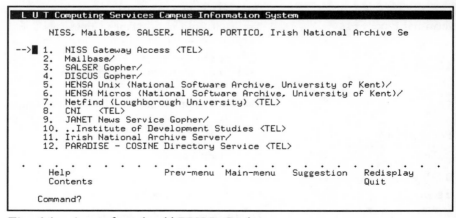

Fig. 6.1   *A page from the old BUBL Gopher*

Table 6.3   Basic procedures for using a Gopher server via telnet or via a command line Gopher client.
(Substitute actual information for items shown in *italics*).

Connecting and disconnecting	
telnet *site-address*	Connect to server via telnet client.
login: gopher	If you do not know the public userid try gopher or the common name of the service at the login: prompt.
gopher *site-address*	Connect to server via Gopher client.

Navigating menus	
u	Move up to previous menu.
↑↓	Move up or down menu items.
number	Jump to specified menu item number.
<space bar>	Display next screen of current menu or text document.
−/+	Move between pages in a menu.
<RETURN key>	Select current item on the menu.
?	Request help.
=	Reveal where a link leads.

Gopher menu items end with codes which tell you what they link to. The main codes are:

/	a menu
.	a text file
<bin>	a binary file
<?>	a searchable index (e.g. WAIS, Veronica)
<TEL>	a telnet session to a different site.

Before choosing a link, it is wise to see where it leads. Normally the '=' character is the command to reveal the link. Links leading to US sites later in the day should be avoided as they will be slow in responding. If your chosen link gives some form of network error (e.g. 'not available') try again some other time.

When searching **Veronica**, you can use **Boolean operators** (AND, OR, NOT) to link search terms. Truncation is indicated by the '*' character. Phrases used as search terms must be enclosed in quotes.

Tips on using WWW

Accessing WWW via telnet

If you do not have a WWW client it is possible to access some publicly accessible WWW browsers via telnet (telnet addresses are given in the resource guide for some such sites). The procedures for browsing can vary enormously, depending on what software is in use at the remote site. Navigating around can be rather confusing to new users. As when using a remote Gopher, always watch the instructions at the bottom of the screen and ensure that you do not miss relevant continuation pages.

The example in Figure 6.2 shows the BUBL WWW server seen using a Lynx browser, which is quite common. Hypertext links are highlighted.

The cursor position is usually shown in inverse video. Notice the use of the arrow keys. Up (↑) and down (↓) arrows are used to move the cursor from one link on a page to the next. This can be up and down the page, or between highlights on the same line. The right arrow (→) or <RETURN> key is used to select the current link (as indicated by the position of the cursor) and the left (←) arrow is used to return to the previous page. It is easy to confuse the use of the up/down and the right/left arrow keys. Remember that up/down arrows are for moving between links on the *same page*; right/left arrow keys are for moving *between pages*.

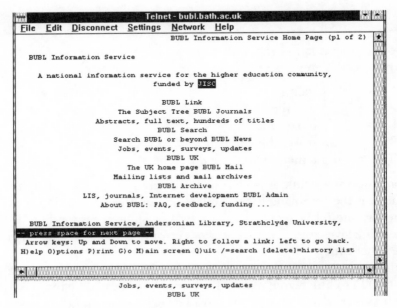

Fig. 6.2 *Telnet to BUBL WWW server seen via Lynx*

Working with URLs

If you have a WWW browser you can 'open' a link to any page on the Internet, providing you know its URL. Use the 'open' command or its equivalent and enter the URL. If you get 'Not found' or a similar error message, first check that you have entered the URL *exactly* as it should be, character for character and case for case. There are no spaces in URLs. If you have not made a mistake, try truncating the URL by omitting characters from the right hand end, up to the rightmost slash (/). For example, instead of :

http://www.vnu.co.uk/vnu/pcw/bob.htm

try using: http://www.vnu.co.uk/vnu/pcw/

If your 'truncated' URL still does not work, keep removing the last portion until you reach the slash that precedes the site name. If this still fails there is no point in truncating further. All truncation is doing is looking for higher-level pages at the site in question. If you find a URL that works, you may be able to follow links to the page you want. However, do be prepared for invalid URLs, for URLs which point to non-existent pages, or for sites which are not available when you want to use them.

You will find that many URLs end in a slash symbol. This means that the page they refer to has a **default** (expected) name, like home.html or index.htm. The names of pages must comply with the file-naming conventions of the computer where they are kept. Thus home.html cannot be stored on a computer running Windows 3.1, as file extensions (.html in this case) can only be up to three letters long on this operating system.

Retrieving non-text files

Some links lead to individual graphics (graphics on pages are called **inline graphics**), or pieces of sound or video. Your browser needs extra software to handle these formats. Most browsers have a customizable list of file extensions which call up an appropriate piece of software (known as a **viewer** or **helper** or **plug-in**) when a file with a certain extension is retrieved. Plug-ins need to be downloaded and installed: a large collection is available from the *Browserwatch Plug-In Plaza*. Whether sound can be heard or not is also dependent on your computer.

Saving pages

There are three ways of recording an interesting page. If you save its URL in your browser's hotlist you can return easily to the page on another occasion. Alternatively, you can store pages on the computer which is running your browser by setting the browser to load pages to disk or using a 'save as' option if your browser has one. Pages which you have loaded to disk can be reloaded later, but saved pages are normally not reusable for browsing. Finally, some browsers allow you to e-mail a page to yourself. If you have a graphical browser, look for these features on buttons or under the menus.

Improving response times

Pages can sometimes take many minutes to load. Speed of page retrieval depends partly on where the page is coming from. Retrieving a page from the USA is often slow compared to a European site and takes longer later in the day. Use a nearby mirror site if you can find one, and choose a time of day that is likely to be quiet at the remote site.

There are two other ways of speeding up page retrieval. The first is to stop your browser loading graphics (there will be a command to do this). Graphics are nice, but take far longer to load than the textual content of pages. The second way to speed things up is to use a **caching proxy**. This is a special computer which stores a copy of the page(s) that you retrieve. If you go back to those pages, or reload them, your browser will load them from the caching proxy computer, and not the original source. You will need to ask your Internet access provider about the availability of a caching proxy.

Using a WWW browser for other tasks

As well as http (**HyperText Transfer Protocol**), your browser can also perform tasks like telnet, FTP, Gopher browsing and reading files stored on your computer. This is done by replacing the http:// task at the beginning of a URL with another task name:

telnet://   opens a telnet connection to a site whose name follows. Your browser will need external telnet software to run the telnet session. This can be called up in the same way as viewers/helpers.

ftp://   opens an FTP session to a site whose name follows. The site name may be followed by a directory path and a filename, to retrieve a specific file. It is advisable to load binary files to disk rather than any other possible method of transferring them. Note that some resources are unavailable by FTP using a WWW browser.

gopher://   opens a Gopher session to a Gopher whose site name follows. The site name may be followed by a path to a particular page which often bears some relation to the menu headings that lead to the same page from the top level menu at the site.

file://   followed by a directory path and a filename retrieves a file from the computer which is running your browser.

Reading e-mail and USENET newsgroups are usually available via a menu within a graphical browser.

Privacy and WWW

Your browser can allow the sites you browse to collect information about you (your home site, e-mail address, name, the computer you are using etc.). If this bothers you then use the *Anonymous Surfing* resource.

Building a WWW page

Building a WWW page is a straightforward task. HTML (HyperText Markup Language) is a set of **tags**, i.e. matched pairs of markers, which delineate particular features on a page. The basic structure of an HTML page is:

```
<HTML>
<HEADER>
<TITLE>Example HTML page</TITLE>
</HEADER>
<BODY>
This is an example HTML page.
</BODY>
</HTML>
```

Figure 6.3 shows what this looks like on screen.

Each tag names the feature it delineates. The effect of a pair of tags is limited to the material between them. Some tags however are unitary; for example <P> marks the end of a paragraph. Tags are clearly explained in *HyperText Markup Language (HTML)*: working and background material.

Markup tags can be added to text by using a text editor or a word processor. Add-ons have been released for leading word processors, to enable them to save material in HTML format. Software is available which converts files from formats like **RTF** (Rich Text Format) to HTML, as are dedicated HTML editors. If you intend to add graphics to your pages then you will need graphic editing and conversion software. Guides to HTML and associated software are referenced in Brian Kelly's handbook entitled *Running a World-Wide Web Service* and in the *WWW FAQ*.

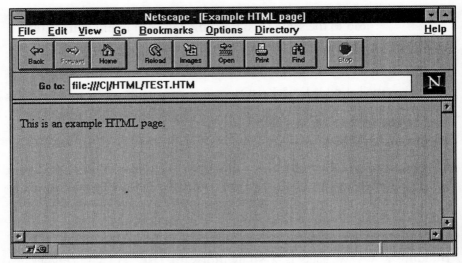

Fig. 6.3   *Display of simple HTML page*

A good way of picking up expertise is to use your browser to view the source (i.e the HTML markup) of any pages which strike you as being well-designed or eye-catching. Remember that your browser can also save retrieved pages in HTML format to the computer on which your browser is running. These can then be examined to see how they work.

It is a good idea to test out your own pages by using your browser to look at your pages as local files (using the file:// task name at the start of the URL). Browsers, though, tend to require the presence of an Internet link to work, so that making a browser work in **local mode** can be tricky.

Making links between your own pages can be a chore if you enter the full URL for each link. **Relative URLs** (usually just a pathname and/or filename) cause your browser to use the root of the last full URL referenced. Thus, if your first page is referenced as:

file://C:/html/home.htm

then another page, stored in the file 'next.htm' in the same directory, only needs to be referenced by the relative URL 'next.htm'. The browser automatically assumes that the full URL is:

file://C:/html/next.htm

You will find that relative links also make your pages easier to move around in file store, without having to change all the URLs that link to them.

If you intend to put your pages on a WWW server for other people to access, try to view your pages first using as many different browsers as you can. You will find that browsers all have idiosyncrasies in the way they render HTML files on screen. Some browsers have various extra tags that they can render; be wary of using these as different browsers cannot interpret them. Finally, consider how your pages look without inline graphics.

Searching the Internet

The Internet is a very new information resource. Many librarians, well-versed in using printed and online/CD-ROM services, have had little experience of Internet searching. There are no clearly defined search strategies nor manuals which document resources. The basic software required is an e-mailer and a WWW browser. A newsreader is an optional extra. Experience and confidence with these is essential. The latest WWW browsers are including e-mail and newsreader facilities.

The Internet should be seen as an addition to the existing range of information sources, yet its very nature makes it unreliable for quick reference work in a library. Even if you know of a site that could contain information to answer a patron's request, and you have the necessary client software to access it, there is no guarantee that the site will be operational, or that your Internet connection will be functioning at the time you need it. Even if things are working, the speed of response might be too slow because of network overload. If you know of an individual, or more likely a discussion list, where an answer to a patron's request might be obtained by e-mail, it is very unlikely that a response will be forthcoming immediately.

So why bother with searching the Internet? It offers a staggering range of data, information and software, covering almost every subject imaginable. The vast majority of this information is free. Because it is free it can be unfavourably compared, for example, with conventional reference books for authority, coverage and consistency but in a sense this is not comparing like with like. The power of the Internet as an information resource lies in information that is not available or not available from the same perspective elsewhere, and, importantly, information that is not easily accessible to the public at large by other means. Its major strength lies in the huge diversity of material available, aimed at all subjects, all levels and all types of user. A vast amount of information has been compiled by enthusiasts, volunteers and interested parties; as an information resource reflecting the spectrum of modern culture, society and human endeavour, the Internet is thus unparalleled. Volunteer information providers (mainly individuals) often include a disclaimer about the accuracy and comprehensiveness of their data, yet the quality *can* be admirable.

Much information is supplied in good faith and may have a copyright notice which sets clear limits on how the data can be used. But usage is almost impossible to police, as users can make their own copy of any information resource. Mainstream publishers are wary of using the Internet for anything more than sales and advertising, through fears of piracy.

Just as the provision of information on the Internet is *ad hoc*, so is its organization for retrieval. The vast majority of information providers on the Internet are not librarians. It shows when one looks for the sort of standardization and consistency in cataloguing, indexing and classification that one takes for granted in libraries. Part of the problem is that existing library standards are not necessarily appropriate, in terms of the material they cover and their usability by non-librarians. Because of this fundamental lack of organization of information, searching the Internet can be a very frustrating activity.

The first thing to decide is whether a traditional source will give you the information you require. The Internet can function as a gateway to library OPACS and to collections of library-based resources (like CARL). However the Internet comes into its own when traditional sources fail.

The basic resources are covered under 'Subject listings and indexes' in the resource guide. The best way to start is to investigate a general subject listing, like *Yahoo* or *BUBL LINK* (which is maintained in DDC order by librarian volunteers) or collections of specific guides to subject resources, like those maintained by the *Clearinghouse of Subject-Oriented Internet Resource Guides* (first produced from project work by library school students and now commercially sponsored). You may be lucky and find sites you can return to again and again or you may spend a lot of time browsing and find nothing suitable.

If browsing fails to turn up anything, then call up a searchable index, like *Lycos*, *AltaVista*, *InfoSeek* or *Hotbot*. Since these are machine-generated indexes they can include more resources than can the subject listings. With no keyword control, however, you are searching a vast amount of free-text; misses and false drops due to the vagaries of word usage are almost inevitable. You need to strike a balance between combining too many search terms and too few. Each searchable index (or **search engine**) differs in the searching facilities it offers. Be sure to read any available help file. Some searchable indexes specialize in indexing particular types of information (like e-mail addresses, newsgroups etc.). Services like *Allinone* and *Search.com* collect and group searchable indexes by category.

Even the machine-generated indexes cannot cover everything. The last resort is asking by e-mail or USENET for either pointers to resources, or just for the information you require. This is the step that takes the most amount of time as you have to identify relevant discussion lists or USENET newsgroups first, and then follow them to make sure that they cover your topic properly and that your question is not a common one. However, if you locate the correct forum, you can be sure to get some sort of an answer to your question. No response probably means that no one knows! When all else fails, the *STUMPERS-L* discussion list is for questions that no one else can answer; it is of course populated by reference librarians!

If searching is arduous for the librarian, then what about end-user searching? The appeal of the Internet for the end-user is that not finding what they want is very often offset by finding something of equal interest that they did not know they wanted. The Internet is also seductively available for the end-user, as it comes to their office or home computer. This is not yet a threat to the library; the Internet contains very different types of information and does not offer access to that information in a straightforward and dependable manner.

How to keep up to date with resources on the Internet

Keeping up to date is essentially a matter of following appropriate discussion lists and USENET newsgroups. You will find that other people announce their own new resources, or recommend ones which they themselves have used. The problem is how to store these recommendations so that you can act on them later, as the need arises or the time becomes available?

If you can locate a couple of information servers that cover your interests, you are in luck. All you need to do is hotlist these sites in your WWW browser and return to them occasionally to check whether they have been updated since your last visit. It is becoming standard practice for the date the page was last updated to appear at the bottom of 'welcome' pages at Web sites. Look for any new resources that you have seen announced on discussion lists and newsgroups, or check out the 'What's new' pages that now appear on many Web servers. If you can find a well-maintained server, then keeping up to date is done for you!

What if you cannot find existing information servers which cover your topics and which are kept up to date? You are then left with raw announcements from discussion lists and newsgroups. Printing these out for future reference is hopeless unless you have all the time in the world to spend filing ephemera. Organizing messages into appropriately named folders on your computer is marginally better, but it is worth being ruthless about deleting anything you have not acted on after a period of time. In all likelihood, the information will have been superseded.

In fact, all you really need to store are e-mail addresses and WWW URLs, as the latter can accommodate all the existing range of Internet file resources. You might also want to add a short explanation for each one.

E-mail or newsgroup postings typically mention only one e-mail address or URL per posting, so it is wasteful to print or save the whole message. Transcribing e-mail addresses and URLs onto paper or into a word-processor involves extra work, and the references may still not be available in a convenient form when you need them, that is when you are online.

The best solution is to learn to build a WWW page in HTML and to use it as a personal repository of up-to-date resources. You do not need a home page on a WWW server to do this. Your WWW browser can retrieve a page stored as a local file on the computer you use to access the Internet. Thus, when online, all your references are immediately available and, if they are URLs, immediately useable as well.

If you think your resource page is worthy enough, then publish it by putting it on a WWW server as a home page. Ask your Internet access provider about access to WWW server space. If you announce your WWW home page through discussion lists and newsgroups, you will find that people will comment on your page, and maybe point out resources that you have missed. They may also let you know by personal e-mail about resources they find. The best way to stay up to date is to become a well-known and well-respected information provider yourself!

PART IV
Internet resource guide

Contents

IV

INTRODUCTION TO PART IV

How to read the resource guide

The resource guide is organized into broad sections which follow the same sequence as the main text. Within each section, resources are arranged alphabetically by name and incorporate everything cited in the main text along with additional resources relevant to the section. To locate useful resources, browse the entries in the appropriate section/s.

If the resource sought has a recognized name, then it will be locatable via the Index to the book.

Each resource is described according to a standard template, an annotated version of which is shown on page 98 to explain the entries in the main guide and how to use them.

Throughout, italics have been used to indicate where you should substitute your own information, such as your name or e-mail address.

For most resources, including information servers and FTP sites, access details are expressed in terms of URLs. If a resource is also (or only) available via telnet, then a site-address and public user identifier (to login via telnet) are also given. Resources were last checked in February 1997. Details may have changed since then.

Interpreting URLs for use with command line Gopher and FTP clients

If you are using a command line FTP client, then you will need to deconstruct the URL to identify the site address. Reading from the left, this immediately follows the double slash, up to (but not including) the next slash. Using this with your client will lead to the root page or directory at a site. The remainder of the URL gives the directory path (or part of it) and usually the filename. For example:

ftp://ftp.lib.berkeley.edu/pub/Current.Cites/OREADME

ftp.lib.berkeley.edu	is the site name (e.g. `ftp ftp.lib.berkeley.edu`)
/pub/Current.Cites/	is the directory path (e.g. `cd pub/Current.Cites/`)
OREADME	is the filename (e.g. `get OREADME`)

Not all URLs for FTP give a filename, or even a full directory path. After connecting to the remote site, you should display the contents of the current directory (for example, using the ls command) to see whether the file you want is there. If not, you may need to move down to a further subdirectory.

NAME[*]   Common abbreviation (if any) and Full name of the resource.

TYPE   Resource type as described in the main text.

ISSN   ISSN for e-journals only.

PROVIDER[*]   Organizational and/or personal name of the provider and (Country in which the resource is located).

DESCRIPTION[*]   Factual description of the resource.

COMMENTS   Impressionistic comments about content, organization or access to the resource.

ACCESS[*]

URL(S)	One or more URLs, giving a UK or European location if available.
	Some resources are available by several methods (http://, ftp:// etc.) in which case, URLs for each are shown.
	(Type URLs into your client on a single line, otherwise *exactly* as they are shown).
TELNET	Site address/es (host and domain name/s).
	IP address may also be given.
	(Use with command line telnet client, e.g.
	`telnet site-address`
	or construct a URL as follows:
	`telnet://site-address/`)
LOGIN	The public user identifier for the remote system.
	(Type this at the login: prompt).
PATH	Menu path to the resource for basic telnet users.
LOGOUT	Disconnect command for basic telnet users.
E-MAIL	E-mail address.
	(If given, send a message to this e-mail address to receive a plain text copy of the resource by e-mail. Leave the subject line blank).
MESSAGE	Text of the message that you should send.

SUBSCRIPTION DETAILS

E-MAIL	E-mail address of mail server for discussion lists and e-journals.
	(Send a message to this e-mail address to subscribe. Leave the subject line blank).
MESSAGE	Text of the message that you should send to subscribe.
	(Substitute your own details for anything in *italics*, e.g. Jane Smith for *your-firstname your-lastname*).
CONTACT DETAILS	e-mail, telephone and/or fax number for further information.

Annotated template, explaining entries in the resource guide.

[*]These elements are present for every resource. The remainder are optional.

Resources linked to Part I

Networking organizations

Name   The Archive, SunSITE Northern Europe FTP archive
Type   Information server; FTP archive
Provider   SunSITE Northern Europe (UK); (Department of Computing, Imperial College, London)
Description   A massive archive of software, USENET newsgroups and FAQs, e-journals, multi-media and more. Lists FTP servers worldwide and provides Archie services. Also provides some links to UK-specific networking information.
Access

URL(s)	http://src.doc.ic.ac.uk/	
	ftp://src.doc.ic.ac.uk/	
Telnet	src.doc.ic.ac.uk	
	193.63.255.1	
Login	sources	(for the archives)
	archie	(for Archie)

Name   Electronic Frontier Foundation
Type   Information server, FTP archive
Provider   EFF – Electronic Frontier Foundation (USA)
Description   The Electronic Frontier Foundation is a civil liberties pressure group for Internet-related issues, like individual privacy and freedom of expression. Its file archives contain a wealth of material on its activities and related areas. It publishes a newsletter, EFFector Online, distributed on the USENET group comp.org.eff.news. The EFF's (Extended) Guide to the Internet is freely available at this site. EFF activities and related issues are debated on the USENET group comp.org.eff.talk.
Comments   A pioneering organisation. Membership is open to interested parties.
Access

URL(s)	http://www.eff.org
	ftp://ftp.eff.org
	news:comp.org.eff.news
	news:comp.org.eff.talk

Contact details

E-mail	ask@eff.org
Tel	+ 1-415-436-9333
Fax	+ 1-415-436-9993

NAME   The Electronic Libraries Programme
TYPE   Information server
PROVIDER   UKOLN
DESCRIPTION   The UK-based Electronic Libraries Programme (eLib) is a major research effort investigating the electronic/digital library. Background to the Programme, and links to all current and past projects are on the web server.
ACCESS

    URL(s)   http://ukoln.bath.ac.uk/elib/

NAME   IETF – Internet Engineering Task Force
TYPE   Information server; FTP archive
PROVIDER   IETF Secretariat (USA and International)
DESCRIPTION   Working under the auspices of the Internet Society, the IETF provides Internet management, standards and technical information, and many sources of further information.
ACCESS

    URL(s)   http://www.ietf.cnri.reston.va.us/
                  ftp://nic.nordu.net/
    E-MAIL   mailserv@ds.internic.net
    MESSAGE   file *required-pathname*
    PATH   *your-email-address*

NAME   InetUK: UK Internet Access Providers
TYPE   Directory, Information server
PROVIDER   ArcGlade Services Ltd
DESCRIPTION   Names, addresses, contact details plus a summary of the services, fees and resources of UK Internet access providers offering any of e-mail, USENET, telnet, FTP (many offer additional Internet-services).
ACCESS

    URL(s)   http://www.limitless.co.uk/inetuk/providers.html
                  ftp://www.limitless.co.uk/pub/inetuk/
    E-MAIL   majordomo@limitless.co.uk
    MESSAGE   get inetuk inetuk.sum

NAME   **Internet Cafe Guide**
TYPE   Information server
PROVIDER   Ernst Larsen
DESCRIPTION   Guide to Internet cafes worldwide. Strong on the UK.
ACCESS
    URL(s)   http://www.netcafeguide.com/

NAME   **Internet Society Home Page**
TYPE   Information server; FTP archive
PROVIDER   Internet Society (USA and International)
DESCRIPTION   Contains information, activities and corporate membership of the Internet Society as well as much information about the Internet (administration, funding, codes of conduct, key organizations, usage statistics).
ACCESS
    URL(s)   http://info.isoc.org/
            ftp://ftp.isoc.org/
CONTACT DETAILS
    E-MAIL   isoc@isoc.org
    TEL   +1-703-648-9888
    FAX   +1-703-648-9887

NAME   **Internet Watch Foundation**
TYPE   Alerting service
PROVIDER   Internet Watch Foundation/Peter Dawe
DESCRIPTION   Dedicated to the removal of illegal material from the Internet. Runs a hotline for reporting such material.
ACCESS
    URL(s)   http://www.internetwatch.org.uk/
CONTACT DETAILS (HOTLINE)
    E-MAIL   report@internetwatch.org.uk
    TEL   01223-236077
    FAX   01223-235921

NAME   **JANET Information Server**
TYPE   Information server
PROVIDER   UKERNA – United Kingdom Educational and Research Networking Association (UK)
DESCRIPTION   Contains a wealth of information and documentation on JANET and SuperJANET including policy and technical documents, JANET sites and servers, major UK National networking facilities. Incorporates the newsletter, JANET.news.
ACCESS

URL(s)	http://www.ja.net/
E-MAIL	infoserv@news.janet.ac.uk
MESSAGE	request index (for an index of documents)
	request *reference-number* (for a specific document number from the index)

CONTACT DETAILS

E-MAIL	service@ukerna.ac.uk
TEL	01235-822212
FAX	01235-822397

NAME   **TERENA – Trans-European Research and Education Networking Association**
TYPE   Information server
PROVIDER   TERENA Secretariat (The Netherlands and Europe)
DESCRIPTION   Information about TERENA and its predecessor, EARN. Also European-wide networking initiatives including reports, calls for proposals, conference papers and abstracts. Also contains documentation for major Internet tools, much of which comes from the former EARN, and links to international networking centres (e.g. InterNic).
ACCESS

URL(s)	http://www.terena.nl/

CONTACT DETAILS

E-MAIL	secretariat@terena.org
TEL	+31-20-639-1131
FAX	+31-20-639-3289

NAME   **UKOLN Information Service**
TYPE   Information server
PROVIDER   UKOLN – The UK Office for Library and Information Networking (UK)
DESCRIPTION   Provides information about UKOLN itself (e.g. research, publications, activities etc.). Has good links to related research activities in networked information retrieval.
ACCESS

URL(S)   http://www.ukoln.bath.ac.uk/
CONTACT DETAILS
TEL   01225-826580
FAX   01225-826838

NAME   **W3C – the World Wide Web Consortium**
TYPE   Information server
PROVIDER   The Laboratory for Computer Science at MIT, INRIA (Institut National de Recherche en Informatique et en Automatique) and Keio University with support from DARPA and the European Commission
DESCRIPTION   The W3C was founded in 1994 to develop common standards for the evolution of the World Wide Web. It is the source for any technical or background information relating to the Web itself. The Director of the W3C is Tim Berners-Lee, the creator of the World Wide Web.
ACCESS

URL(S)   http://www.w3.org/
TELNET   telnet.w3.org

Resources linked to Part II

DISCUSSION LISTS AND ELECTRONIC CONFERENCES

NAME   Deja News – the Source for Internet Newsgroups
TYPE   Information server
PROVIDER   Deja News Inc (USA)
DESCRIPTION   Has the largest collection of archived USENET newsgroups, with coverage going back to March 1995.
ACCESS

> **URL(s)**   http://www.dejanews.com/

NAME   Directory of Scholarly Electronic Conferences
TYPE   Directory
PROVIDER   Diane K. Kovacs and team, Kent State University Libraries (USA)
DESCRIPTION   Provides descriptions and subscription information of approaching 2000 academic discussion lists and newsgroups, listed by subject category. Descriptions can also be searched by keyword.
COMMENTS   Includes a large number of established lists in the library and information sector, including UK lists on Mailbase. A plain text version of the directory, in alphabetical order by list name, can be retrieved by sending one of the specified e-mail messages to the listserv address below.
ACCESS

> **URL(s)**   http://n2h2.com/KOVACS/
> **E-MAIL**   listserv@kentvm.kent.edu
> **MESSAGE**   get acadlist.library f=mail (for the library and
> information science section)
> get acadlist.readme f=mail (for instructions and
> an index of other sections)

NAME   Discussion Lists: Mailing List Manager Commands
TYPE   Full text document
PROVIDER   James Milles, Saint Louis University Law Library (USA)
DESCRIPTION   Summary of commands for five widely used mail server programs used to manage Internet discussion lists: Listserv, Listproc, Mailbase, Mailserv and Majordomo.
ACCESS

> **URL(s)**   http://lawlib.slu.edu/training/mailser.htm
> **E-MAIL**   listserv@listserv.acsu.buffalo.edu
> **MESSAGE**   get mailser cmd nettrain

NAME   European MBONE FAQ
TYPE   Full text document
PROVIDER   RIPE Mbone Working Group
DESCRIPTION   European edition of the Multicast Backbone (Mbone) Frequently Asked Questions (FAQ) and their answers.
ACCESS

> **URL(s)**   http://surver.wind.surfnet.nl/~bos/mbone-eufaq.html

NAME   Index of /usenet/
TYPE   Information server; USENET archive
PROVIDER   SunSITE Northern Europe (UK), (Department of Computing, Imperial College, London)
DESCRIPTION   The largest archive of USENET postings and FAQs in the UK, listed by group and by USENET category.
ACCESS

> **URL(s)**   http://src.doc.ic.ac.uk/usenet/
> ftp://src.doc.ic.ac.uk/usenet/
> **TELNET**   src.doc.ic.ac.uk
> **LOGIN**   sources
> **PATH**   /usenet/
> **LOGOUT**   logout

NAME   Internet Public Library MOO
TYPE   Text-based MOO
PROVIDER   School of Information and Library Studies, University of Michigan (USA)
DESCRIPTION   An experimental MOO, aiming to provide an interactive public library environment where 'librarians and information seekers can gather together, talk and provide reference services'.
COMMENTS   The WWW server gives information and instructions. To participate, connect via telnet.
ACCESS

> **URL(s)**   http://ipl.sils.umich.edu/ref/MOO/
> **TELNET**   ipl.sils.umich.edu
> **LOGIN**   iplmoo
> **LOGOUT**   @quit

NAME   Library-Oriented Lists and Electronic Serials
TYPE   Directory
PROVIDER   Steve Bonario and Ann Thornton, University of Houston (USA)
DESCRIPTION   A full-text document listing a considerable number of BIT-NET and Internet lists and e-journals in the library and information sector, giving target audience for each and brief instructions for subscribing.
COMMENTS   Includes Listserv, Listproc and other Types of list, but not Mailbase. Can be retrieved by e-mailing the listserv address given below. The Web server provides a useful subject index and indicates which lists can be read as USENET newsgroups.
ACCESS

URL(S)	http://info.lib.uh.edu/liblists/liblists.htm
E-MAIL	listserv@uhupvm1.uh.edu
MESSAGE	get library lists f=mail

NAME   LIS-link
TYPE   Discussion list (unmoderated)
PROVIDER   Mailbase (UK)
DESCRIPTION   Generally recognised as the key list for news, announcements and discussion of general interest to the UK library and information community. Postings cover wide-ranging topics within the general sphere of library and information work. Used by BUBL to distribute regular update bulletins.
ACCESS

URL(S)	http://www.mailbase.ac.uk/lists/lis-link/

SUBSCRIPTION DETAILS

E-MAIL	mailbase@mailbase.ac.uk
MESSAGE	join LIS-link *your-firstname your-lastname*

NAME   LISTSERV List-of-Lists
TYPE   Directory
PROVIDER   Various
DESCRIPTION   A listing of all Listserv lists by name with brief descriptions.
ACCESS

E-MAIL	listserv@lsoft.com (or any other Listserv)
MESSAGE	list global (for all lists)
LIST GLOBAL	keyword (for lists on a topic)

NAME   **LISTSERV User Guide**
TYPE   Information server, Full text document
PROVIDER   EARN Association (Europe)
DESCRIPTION   Full instructions for locating, using and setting up LISTSERV lists.
ACCESS

URL(s)	http://www.earn.net/lug/notice.html
E-MAIL	listserv@earncc.earn.net
MESSAGE	get lsvguide memo (ASCII text)
	get lsvguide ps (Postscript)

NAME   **Liszt , the mailing list directory**
TYPE   Information server; Directory
PROVIDER   Scott Southwick (USA)
DESCRIPTION   Searchable directory of over 65,000 mailing lists, updated weekly.
ACCESS

URL(s)	http://www.liszt.com/
E-MAIL	liszter@bluemarble.net
MESSAGE	help (for listing of search commands)

NAME   **Mailbase Mailing List Service**
TYPE   Information server; Discussion list archive
PROVIDER   Mailbase (UK)
DESCRIPTION   Provides a complete alphabetical listing of all Mailbase discussion lists, with further information including joining instructions, owners and moderators, members and mail archives for each list. Also Mailbase documentation including instructions for setting up a list.
COMMENTS   As list names are seldom meaningful, the alphabetical index is only useful to locate information about a known list. However, there is an index of list names and descriptions to search for lists on a topic. It is also possible to search the membership of all Mailbase lists to locate a person's e-mail address, and to search the archives of a specified list.
ACCESS

URL(s)	http://www.mailbase.ac.uk/

CONTACT DETAILS

E-MAIL	mailbase-helpline@mailbase.ac.uk
TEL	0191-2228080
FAX	0191-2228580

NAME New-List
TYPE Mailing list (moderated)
PROVIDER Marty Hoag, NDSU Information Technology Services (USA)
DESCRIPTION Informs subscribers of new Listserv lists as they are created.
SUBSCRIPTION DETAILS
    E-MAIL listserv@vm1.nodak.edu
    MESSAGE subscribe new-list *your-firstname your-lastname*

NAME New-Lists
TYPE Mailing list (moderated)
PROVIDER Mailbase (UK)
DESCRIPTION Informs subscribers of new Mailbase lists as they are created.
ACCESS
    URL(s) http://www.mailbase.ac.uk/lists/new-lists/
SUBSCRIPTION DETAILS
    E-MAIL mailbase@mailbase.ac.uk
    MESSAGE join new-lists *your-firstname your-lastname*

NAME Network News
TYPE USENET FAQ archive
PROVIDER University of Oxford (UK)
DESCRIPTION A major UK repository of USENET newsgroup FAQs, listed by name and by category. The archive can also be searched by keyword.
ACCESS
    URL(s) http://www.lib.ox.ac.uk/internet/news/

NAME PACS-L The Public-Access Computer Systems Forum
TYPE Electronic conference; Discussion list
PROVIDERS Dana Rooks, Gretchen McCord Hoffman, Linda Thompson, University of Houston (USA)
DESCRIPTION One of the largest library-oriented lists, PACS-L handles discussion on end-user computer systems of all Types of libraries. Subscribers also receive Current Cites, PACS-News, PACS-Review and the LITA Newsletter (Electronic Journals).
ACCESS
    URL(s) http://info.lib.uh.edu/pacsl.html
SUBSCRIPTION DETAILS
    E-MAIL listserv@uhupvm1.uh.edu
    MESSAGE subscribe pacs-l *your-firstname your-lastname*

NAME **PAML – Publicly Accessible Mailing Lists**
TYPE Information server; Directory
PROVIDER Stephanie da Silva (USA)
DESCRIPTION A massive, multidisciplinary collection of discussion lists, arranged by name and by subject keywords on the WWW server.
ACCESS
  URL(s) http://www.NeoSoft.com/internet/paml/
  ftp://rtfm.mit.edu/pub/usenet/news.answers
  /mail/mailing-lists/part01 [-22]

NAME **STUMPERS-L**
TYPE Discussion list
PROVIDER Concordia University (USA)
DESCRIPTION Challenging reference questions (a list for librarians only).
ACCESS
  URL(s) http://www.cuis.edu/~stumpers/intro.html
SUBSCRIPTION DETAILS
  E-MAIL mailserv@crf.cuis.edu
  MESSAGE subscribe stumpers-l your-e-mailaddress

NAME **TILE.NET**
TYPE Information server; Directory
PROVIDER Walter Shelby Group Ltd (USA)
DESCRIPTION Complete index to USENET newsgroups, Listserv discussion lists (and FTP sites), listed by name and by category. Gives a short description of each group, brief usage statistics and access details (where known).
ACCESS
  URL(s) http://tile.net/

NAME **Zippo Dot Com**
TYPE Information server
PROVIDER Zippo Dot Com, Inc (USA)
DESCRIPTION Provides free access to 4,500 USENET newsgroups via a friendly web-based interface. More newsgroups are available via subscription.
ACCESS
  URL(s) http://www.zippo.com/
  http://drn.zippo.com/news-bin/wwwnews?
  newsgroup name (for direct access to a
  newsgroup)

ELECTRONIC JOURNALS, NEWSLETTERS AND ALERTING SERVICES

NAME **Ariadne**
TYPE Electronic newsletter; Printed newsletter
PROVIDER University Library, University of Abertay Dundee, and UKOLN
DESCRIPTION Bi-monthly newsletter aiming to cover sources and services on the Internet of relevance to librarians, especially the Electronic Libraries Programme (eLib). Available also in printed form, but the Web version contains additional material.
ACCESS
      URL(s) http://ukoln.bath.ac.uk/ariadne/
CONTACT DETAILS
      E-MAIL ariadne@ukoln.bath.ac.uk

NAME **BUBL Journals**
TYPE Information server
PROVIDER BUBL Information Service (UK)
DESCRIPTION BUBL itself holds a collection of electronic journals and provides links to major repositories elsewhere. There are also links to directories of e-journals.
ACCESS
      URL(s) http://bubl.ac.uk/journals
      TELNET bubl.bath.ac.uk
      LOGIN bubl
      PATH BUBL Journals
      LOGOUT q

NAME **CAUSE/EFFECT**
TYPE Electronic newsletter; printed newsletter
PROVIDER CAUSE
DESCRIPTION Quarterly newsletter for managers and users of information resources in higher education. Also available in printed form.
ACCESS
      URL(s) http://cause-www.niss.ac.uk/cause-effect/
              cause-effect.html

NAME   **Current Cites**
TYPE   Alerting service (monthly)
ISSN 1060-2356
PROVIDER   University of California, Berkeley Library (USA)
DESCRIPTION   Provides citations and brief annotations to selected articles from over 30 library and information technology journals (hard copy and electronic) covering optical disc technologies, networks, electronic publishing, hypermedia and multimedia.
ACCESS

    URL(s)   http://www.lib.ncsu.edu/stacks/currentc/
                            ftp://ftp.lib.berkeley.edu/pub/Current.Cites/

SUBSCRIPTION DETAILS
    E-MAIL   listserv@library.berkeley.edu
    MESSAGE   sub cites *yourname*
    NOTE   Sent automatically to PACS-L and PACS-P subscribers.

NAME   **D-Lib**
TYPE   Electronic newsletter
PROVIDER   Defence Advanced Research Projects Agency (DARPA) (USA)
DESCRIPTION   Monthly newsletter reporting on digital library research, especially that from the NSF/DARPA/NASA Digital Library Initiative in the USA.
ACCESS

    URL(s)   http://ukoln.bath.ac.uk/dlib/magazine.html
                            http://www.dlib.org/

NAME   **DeLiberations**
TYPE   Electronic newsletter
PROVIDER   Educational and Staff Development Unit, London Guildhall University
DESCRIPTION   For educational developers, librarians and academic staff involved in teaching and learning in higher education. Does not have regular issues but is continually updated.
ACCESS

    URL(s)   http://www.lgu.ac.uk/deliberations/

NAME Directory of Electronic Journals, Newsletters and Academic Discussion Lists

TYPE Directory

PROVIDER Association of Research Libraries (USA)

DESCRIPTION One of the most extensive, multidisciplinary listings of electronic journals etc. on the Internet. Also available for sale in printed format (from the contact given below).

COMMENTS Electronic journals and newsletters are listed alphabetically by title in two separate sections on the information server (text file). The sections can be searched collectively by keyword. The e-journal section has evolved from the well-known directory first produced by Michael Strangelove at the University of Ottawa. The server also links to the 'Directory of Scholarly Electronic Conferences', compiled by Diane Kovacs and team at Kent State University.

ACCESS

        URL(S) http://arl.cni.org/scomm/edir/

CONTACT DETAILS

        E-MAIL pubs@cni.org

NAME Internet Resources Newsletter

TYPE Electronic newsletter; Directory

ISSN 1361-9381

PROVIDER Heriot-Watt University, Internet Resource Centre

DESCRIPTION Monthly newsletter aiming to raise awareness of selected new resources and services on the Internet.

ACCESS

        URL(S) http://www.hw.ac.uk/libWWW/irn/irn.html

NAME NewJour

TYPE mailing list

PROVIDER Ann Shumelda Okerson (Yale University) and James J. O'Donnell (University of Pennsylvania)

DESCRIPTION List for receiving announcements of electronic journals as they become available. The archive of past announcements is searchable.

ACCESS

        URL(S) http://gort.ucsd.edu/newjour/

SUBSCRIPTION DETAILS

        E-MAIL listserv@ccat.sas.upenn.edu

        MESSAGE subscribe NewJour

NAME **Library-Oriented Lists and Electronic Serials**
(see entry in Discussion lists and electronic conferences)

NAME **PACS-P (Public Access Computer Systems Publications)**
TYPE Mailing list
PROVIDER University of Houston Libraries (USA)
DESCRIPTION Subscribers receive all four PACS-L publications (Current Cites, PACS-News, PACS-Review, LITA Newsletter), but not the PACS-L discussions.
ACCESS
    URL(S) http://info.lib.uh.edu/pacsp.html
SUBSCRIPTION DETAILS
    E-MAIL listserv@uhupvm1.uh.edu
    MESSAGE subscribe pacs-p *your-firstname your-lastname*

NAME **Public-Access Computer Systems News**
TYPE Electronic newsletter
ISSN 1050-6004
PROVIDER University of Houston Libraries (USA)
DESCRIPTION Established in 1990, PACS News is published irregularly with news items related to end-user computer systems in libraries.
COMMENTS Although many news items originate in the USA, this is a useful newsletter for library software products and system updates. Back issues are available, but only listed by volume and issue.
ACCESS
    URL(S) http://info.lib.uh.edu/pacsnews.html
SUBSCRIPTION DETAILS
    NOTE Sent automatically to PACS-L and PACS-P subscribers.

NAME   The Public Access Computer Systems Review
TYPE   Electronic journal (refereed)
ISSN   1048-6542
PROVIDER   Charles W. Bailey, Jr. (Editor-in-Chief), University of Houston Libraries (USA
DESCRIPTION   Established in 1989. Publishes articles concerning all aspects of end-user computer systems in libraries. Distributed free of charge via the Internet, with its first five volumes now available in hard copy from American Library Association Library and Information Technology Services.
COMMENTS   Articles can be received automatically by subscribing to PACS-P, or retrieved selectively via the server. Subject and author indexes and author guidelines are also available on the server.
ACCESS
   URL(S)   http://info.lib.uh.edu/pacsrev.html

NAME   Scholarly Journals Distributed via the Web
TYPE   Information server; Directory
PROVIDER   Charles W. Bailey, Jr., University of Houston Libraries (USA)
DESCRIPTION   An alphabetic, multidisciplinary listing by title, carrying links to but no further information about each one.
ACCESS
   URL(S)   http://info.lib.uh.edu/wj/webjour.html

NAME   Scout Report Homepage
TYPE   Information server
PROVIDER   Net Scout Services (USA)
DESCRIPTION   Weekly publication of the InterNIC Net Scout project at the University of Wisconsin – Madison, intended to inform researchers and educators of new valuable resources on the Internet.
ACCESS
   URL(S)   http://rs.internic.net/scout_report-index.html
   E-MAIL   listserv@lists.internic.net
   MESSAGE   subscribe scout-report

NAME The World-Wide Web Virtual Library: Electronic Journals
Catalog
TYPE Information server; Directory
PROVIDER E-Doc (USA)
DESCRIPTION A relatively small catalogue, but does include e-journals aimed
at a general and commercial readership as well as academic.
ACCESS

        URL(S) http://www.edoc.com/ejournal/

GENERAL REFERENCE WORKS

NAME   **Britannica Online**
TYPE   Information server
PROVIDER   Britannica Advanced Publishing, Inc. (USA)
DESCRIPTION   A trial version of the Encyclopaedia Britannica. The full version is only available by subscription.
ACCESS
>   **URL(s)**   http://www.eb.com/

NAME   **Dictionaries and Reference Works on HUMBUL**
TYPE   Information server
PROVIDER   University of Oxford (UK)
DESCRIPTION   A good selection of general and foreign language dictionaries, quotations, acronyms plus Roget's thesaurus.
ACCESS
>   **URL(s)**   http://info.ox.ac.uk/departments/humanities/
>   dic.html

NAME   **On-line reference works**
TYPE   Directory
PROVIDER   Carnegie Mellon University (USA)
DESCRIPTION   A small but useful compilation of reference works including dictionaries of various types, Internet resource guides and indexes. Other reference material (e.g. maps, gazetteers, phone books, government and legal information, census data) is predominantly US-related.
ACCESS
>   **URL(s)**   http://www.cs.cmu.edu/Web/references.html

NAME   **THOR+: The Virtual Reference Desk**
TYPE   Information server
PROVIDER   The Libraries of Purdue University (USA)
DESCRIPTION   A good composite collection of reference pages from other US academic library servers plus dictionaries and other reference works.
ACCESS
>   **URL(s)**   http://thorplus.lib.purdue.edu/reference/

NAME   **The World Wide Web Acronym and Abbreviation Server**
TYPE   Information server
PROVIDER   University of Cork College (Ireland)
DESCRIPTION   A searchable index of acronyms and their expansions across a wide range of subjects.
ACCESS
URL(S)   http://www.ucc.ie/info/net/acronyms/

NAME   **Yahoo! – Reference**
TYPE   Information server
PROVIDER   Yahoo Inc (USA)
DESCRIPTION   Links to a good selection of general reference works.
ACCESS
URL(S)   http://www.yahoo.co.uk/Reference
http://www.yahoo.com/Reference

NETWORKING GUIDES AND TRAINING MATERIALS

NAME   **CNIDR Home Page**
TYPE   Information server
PROVIDER   The Centre for Networked Information Discovery and Retrieval (USA)
DESCRIPTION   CNIDR provides support for WAIS, WWW, Gopher and emerging Internet applications. The server provides software, reports and other documentation from CNIDR, including free WAIS, a Z39.50 and WHOIS++ gateway server.
ACCESS
        URL(s)   http://cnidr.org/

NAME   **The Guide to Network Resource Tools**
TYPE   Full text document
PROVIDER   TERENA – Trans European Research and Academic Network Association (Netherlands and Europe)
DESCRIPTION   Clearly written guides to major tools including Gopher, WWW, WAIS, Archie, Hytelnet, WHOIS, X.500, Listserv, Mailbase and USENET. As well as giving an overview of each tool, the guide incorporates details of availability (local and remote clients), intended audience, basic usage and examples.
COMMENTS   Being restructured at the time of writing.
ACCESS
        URL(s)   http://www.terena.nl/libr/gnrt/

NAME   **IETF/TERENA Training Materials Catalogue**
TYPE   Information server; Directory
PROVIDER   IETF/TERENA
DESCRIPTION   Aims to catalogue quality materials which can be used to provide Internet training. Includes links to network-accessible materials, and e-mail or offline addresses for ordering the remainder.
COMMENTS   Materials range from videotapes to 'Internet hunts' and cover other academic networks besides the Internet.
ACCESS
        URL(s)   http://www.trainmat.ietf.org/catalogue.html

NAME   **InterNic Directory of Databases and Services**
TYPE   Information server; Directory; FTP archive
PROVIDER   AT & T (USA)
DESCRIPTION   Set up with support from the National Science Foundation, this is a central repository for information about the Internet from the NSF, Internet Society and more. Provides information about and access to major generic search and directory services such as WAIS, Archie, WHOIS, X.500 directory and Netfind.
COMMENTS   Incorporates a 'Directory of Directories' providing good descriptions of Internet resources, with gopher and Web links being added, but dominated by US resources. The directory is WAIS searchable, and browsable by subject and resource type. There are also a number of public access data files containing Internet information. UK users will find some overlapping networking information closer to home (e.g. the Guide to Network Resource Tools from TERENA). This site is overwhelming for new users and document titles can be uninformative.
ACCESS

URL(s)	http://www.internic.net/ds/dspg01.html
	ftp://ftp.internic.net/pub/internic-info/
TELNET	ds.internic.net
LOGIN	guest

NAME   **Netskills**
TYPE   Information server
PROVIDER   University Computing Service, University of Newcastle
DESCRIPTION   Netskills aims to help the UK higher education community make effective use of the Internet for teaching, research and administration. A great collection of training packages, notably TONIC (The Online Netskills Interactive Tutorial), courses, etc.
ACCESS

URL(s)	http://www.netskills.ac.uk/

CONTACT DETAILS

EMAIL	netskills-admin@netskills.ac.uk
TEL	0191-2225000
FAX	0191-2225001

NAME   **Roadmap Internet Training Lessons**

TYPE   Full text document

PROVIDER   Patrick Douglas Crispen

DESCRIPTION   Of the extensive collection of Internet training materials this has been selected as a good, beginners' guide containing easy-to-follow lessons on most of the major Internet tools (e-mail, telnet, FTP, Veronica, Gopher, WWW, etc.).

ACCESS

        URL(S)   http://www.ntu.ac.uk/ess/hallam/roadmap/welcome.html

                         http://ua1vm.ua.edu/~crispen/roadmap.html

SOFTWARE

NAME   The Archive, SunSITE Northern Europe
TYPE   Software archive
(see entry in ' Networking organizations')

NAME   BIBSOFT – Bibliographic Software Listserv
TYPE   Discussion list
PROVIDER   Ruth Lilly Medical Library (USA)
DESCRIPTION   Contains discussions on bibliographic software, and also personal bibliographic software tools (e.g. Pro-Cite, End Note, Reference Manager).
ACCESS

> **E-MAIL**   listserv@listserv.iupui.edu
> **MESSAGE**   subscribe bibsoft

NAME   EMWAC – European Microsoft Windows NT Academic Centre
TYPE   Information server; Software archive
PROVIDER   Datalink Computers, Digital, Microsoft, Research Machines, Sequent and the University of Edinburgh
DESCRIPTION   Comprehensive information on Microsoft products and services including a rich archive of software utilities, documentation, booklists, support service information and details of applications software which runs under Windows. Also an 'Internet toolchest' containing server applications on the Windows NT platform. Acts as a mirror site for other hardware and software houses e.g. Digital, Netscape.
ACCESS

> **URL(s)**   http://www.emwac.ed.ac.uk/
>   ftp://emwac.ed.ac.uk/

CONTACT DETAILS

> **E-MAIL**   emwac@ed.ac.uk

NAME   HENSA – The Higher Education National Software Archives

TYPE   Software archive

PROVIDER   Lancaster University Information Services (UK), University of Kent (UK)

DESCRIPTION   Microcomputer software plus material from CHEST and the CTI Centres, all available free-of-charge to anyone in a UK Higher Education establishment.

COMMENTS   Software is mostly public domain and shareware covering a wide range of applications but especially networking. The archive of microcomputer software is at Lancaster, and the Unix archive at Kent.

ACCESS

   URL(s)   http://www.hensa.ac.uk/
                  ftp://micros.hensa.ac.uk/
                  ftp://unix.hensa.ac.uk/

NAME   IFLA Internet and Library Software Archive

TYPE   Software archive

PROVIDER   International Federation of Library Associations (Canada)

DESCRIPTION   Aims to provide a careful selection of the 'best' software resources to assist librarians using the Internet. The emphasis will be on client software for MS-Windows and Macintosh machines and will include library-specific as well as generic Internet applications and utilities. Provides links to several other software archives

ACCESS

   URL(s)   http://ifla.inist.fr/II/software.htm
                  http://www.nlc-bnc.ca/ifla/II/software.htm

CONTACT DETAILS

   E-MAIL   ifla@nlc-bnc.ca

NAME   Internet Explorer UK mirror

TYPE   Information server; Software archive

PROVIDER   Microsoft, Demon Internet

DESCRIPTION   Contains the latest version of Microsoft's Internet Explorer for Windows platforms and Macintosh.

ACCESS

   URL(s)   http://www.ie.demon.co.uk/
                  http://www.microsoft.com/ie/

NAME   NCSA Mosaic Home Page
TYPE   Information server; Software archive
PROVIDER   NCSA – National Centre for Supercomputing Applications (USA)
DESCRIPTION   Provides NCSA Mosaic client software for Windows, Apple Macintosh and X Windows along with considerable documentation and help on using the Web.
ACCESS
        URL(s)   http://www.ncsa.uiuc.edu/SDG/Software/Mosaic/

NAME   Netscape
TYPE   Information server; Software archive
PROVIDER   Netscape Communications Corporation (USA)
DESCRIPTION   Software archive, commercial product details, demo versions, documentation and support from Netscape.
ACCESS
        URL(s)   http://home.netscape.com/comprod/mirror/
                            client_download.html
                            http://home.netscape.com/comprod/mirror/
                            manual_download.html

NAME   A Survey of Bibliographic Tools
TYPE   Software directory; Information server
PROVIDER   Dana Jacobsen, ACM (USA)
DESCRIPTION   Brief details of bibliographic software tools (format converters, personal bibliographic software, etc.) with some evaluative and explanatory text, references and links to sites for cataloguing information.
ACCESS
        URL(s)   http://www.ecst.csuchico.edu/~jacobsd/bib/tools/

NAME   Shareware.com
TYPE   Software archive; Searchable index
PROVIDER   CNET, Inc
DESCRIPTION   A massive composite archive, approaching 190,000 files, of freeware, shareware, demos, fixes, patches and upgrades. The service provides a search engine (vsl) to search software descriptions. Searches can be restricted to a particular software platform.
ACCESS
        URL(s)   http://www.shareware.com

INFORMATION SERVERS AND GATEWAYS

NAME   **BUBL Information Service**
TYPE   Information server
PROVIDER   BUBL (UK)
DESCRIPTION   BUBL acts as both an information service for the library and
information professions, and as gateway to Internet resources for the
wider academic and research community. As an information service for
LIS it includes abstracts and contents pages of a wide selection of LIS and
IT journals, news of library research and education, meetings, jobs, new
books etc. – with a predominantly UK focus. As a gateway, it provides
links to an overwhelming number of Internet resources in the UK and
worldwide, including electronic journals and texts, worldwide OPACs
(via Hytelnet), major networking tools, software and training materials.
ACCESS

URL(s)	http://bubl.ac.uk/
TELNET	bubl.bath.ac.uk
	138.38.32.45
LOGIN	bubl
LOGOUT	q

NAME   **CLIP – Croydon Libraries Internet Project**
TYPE   Information server
PROVIDER   Croydon Public Library Service (UK)
DESCRIPTION   Includes a link to Croydon Online, the first (experimental)
UK Freenet.
ACCESS

URL(s)	http://www.croydon.gov.uk/cliphome.html

NAME   **Guide to Select BBS's on the Internet**
TYPE   Information server; Directory
PROVIDER   Richard S. Mark (USA)
DESCRIPTION   An extensive alphabetic listing of (mostly US) commercial
and free telnet-accessible bulletin boards. Includes telnet addresses,
URLs and brief descriptions.
ACCESS

URL(s)	http://dkeep.com/sbi.htm
E-MAIL	info@dkmail.dkeep.com
SUBJECT	SBI
MESSAGE	none needed

NAME **European Home Page**
TYPE Information server
PROVIDER Jose Miranda (Portugal)
DESCRIPTION A European map with links to sensitive maps of Web sites in many European countries.
COMMENTS Unsurprisingly, some sites are disappointing, but nevertheless a useful starting point to locate local European resources ranging from popular to research and commercial, arranged by region.
ACCESS
      URL(s)   http://s700.uminho.pt/europa.html

NAME **Free-Nets and Community Networks**
TYPE Information server
PROVIDER Peter Scott, University of Saskatchewan (Canada)
DESCRIPTION FreeNet WWW and telnet sites by country plus related discussion lists and newsgroups.
ACCESS
      URL(s)   http://duke.usask.ca/~scottp/free.html

NAME **NISS Information Gateway**
TYPE Information server
PROVIDER NISS – National Information Services and Systems (UK)
DESCRIPTION Aimed at the UK higher education community, and with a wealth of information from and about it, NISS is also a major national gateway to key, selected network services of all Type s including OPACs, CWIS, subject resources, news sources, information technology guides and more. NISS aims to include resources and information which are reliable and of real value to the academic community.
ACCESS
      URL(s)   http://www.niss.ac.uk/
      TELNET   niss.ac.uk
                193.63.76.1
CONTACT DETAILS
      E-MAIL   niss@niss.ac.uk
      TEL   01225-826036
      FAX   01225-826177

NAME   Sensitive Maps
TYPE   Information server
PROVIDER   School of Computing and Information Technology, University of Wolverhampton (UK)
DESCRIPTION   Interactive maps and guides to a wealth of UK sites including all UK universities, colleges with Web sites, research council funded sites and other sites of general academic and cultural interest that are not directly associated with universities and colleges.
ACCESS
          URL(S)   http://scitsc.wlv.ac.uk/ukinfo/uk.map.html

NAME   UK Guide
TYPE   Information server
PROVIDER   M. Handley, Computer Science Department, University of London (UK)
DESCRIPTION   A bold attempt to provide a guide to the UK, with an emphasis on tourism, travel, recreation and entertainment. There are also links to other Web servers in a number of UK towns and cities, including non-academic and government servers.
COMMENTS   Inevitably the service only provides a snapshot for parts of the UK but it is nonetheless a worthy and interesting example with some useful links.
ACCESS
          URL(S)   http://www.cs.ucl.ac.uk/misc/uk/intro.html

NAME   United Kingdom Based WWW Servers
TYPE   Information server
PROVIDER   SunSITE Northern Europe (UK), (Department of Computing, Imperial College, London)
DESCRIPTION   Lists UK Web servers alphabetically by name under five broad headings (Academic, Commercial, Government, Recreation, Miscellaneous) and also by town/city. This is the UK subset of the major Worldwide list of W3 Servers maintained at CERN (Switzerland).
ACCESS
          URL(S)   http://src.doc.ic.ac.uk/all-uk.html

NAME   **W3 Servers**

TYPE   Information server

PROVIDER   W3C Consortium (International)

DESCRIPTION   The major, international registry of WWW sites listed by continent, country and state.

COMMENTS   Compiled from details submitted by sites who choose to register with this and related national centres. The UK section is maintained at Imperial College, London (see United Kingdom Based WWW Servers).

ACCESS

URL(S)	http://www.w3.org/hypertext/DataSources/WWW/Servers.html
TELNET	www0.cern.ch
	128.141.201.214
PATH	Places to start exploring[3], List of servers[3]

SUBJECT LISTINGS AND INDEXES

NAME   Access to Networked Resources Projects
TYPE   Information server
PROVIDER   UKOLN
DESCRIPTION   Lists the eLib projects aimed at producing subject-specific 'gateways' to Internet resources. Included are:- ADAM (art, design, architecture and media), biz/ed (business education), CAIN (conflict studies), EEVL (engineering), IHR-Info (history), OMNI (medicine), RUDI (urban design) and SOSIG (social sciences).
ACCESS
    URL(s)   http://ukoln.bath.ac.uk/elib/lists/anr.html

NAME   All-in-One Search Page
TYPE   Searchable index
PROVIDER   William Cross
DESCRIPTION   An exhaustive listing of forms-based search tools assembled on one page for easy access. Search tools are categorised under headings (WWW, people, software, news/weather, publications, documentation etc).
ACCESS
    URL(s)   http://www.albany.net/allinone/

NAME   AltaVista Main Page
TYPE   Searchable index
PROVIDER   Digital Equipment Corp. (USA)
DESCRIPTION   Gives access to a searchable database of over 31 million web pages and 4 million USENET postings. Boolean operators are supported, searches can be limited to parts of web pages or USENET postings and advanced options allow features like preferential weighting of certain search words.
ACCESS
    URL(s)   http://www.altavista.telia.com/cgi-bin/telia?
                     country=gb&lang=gb
                     http://www.altavista.digital.com/

Name   Archie
Type   Searchable index
Provider   SunSITE Northern Europe (UK), Imperial College, London
Access

URL(s)	http://src.doc.ic.ac.uk/archieplexform.html
Telnet	src.doc.ic.ac.uk
Login	archie
Logout	q
Note	prog *searchterm* searches for the specified term

Name   **BUBL LINK: Libraries of Networked Knowledge**
Type   Information server
Provider   BUBL Information Service (UK)
Description   An extensive subject tree pointing to resources on BUBL and worldwide. The resource lists are compiled by a growing number of volunteers at different sites, with the intention of providing a service to academics and researchers as well as to librarians.
Comments   Subject tree is arranged by (d)DC classification number, and subject headings can be searched by keyword. Alternatively, subjects are listed alphabetically.
Access

URL(s)	http://bubl.ac.uk/link/
Telnet	bubl.bath.ac.uk
Login	bubl
Path	BUBL Link
Logout	q

Name   **Clearinghouse of Subject-Oriented Internet Resource Guides**
Type   Information server
Provider   Argos Associates, Inc. (USA)
Description   Acts as a repository for subject resource guides compiled by members of the Internet community and by students of the School of Information and Library Studies at the University of Michigan.
Comments   Offers hierachical subject browsing and keyword searching.
Access

URL(s)	http://www.clearinghouse.net/

NAME   HotBot
TYPE   Searchable index
PROVIDER   Hotwired
DESCRIPTION   Gives access to a searchable database of some 54 million web pages. Searches can contain Boolean operators and may be limited to parts of web pages. Searching of USENET postings is also offered.
ACCESS
        URL(s)   http://www.hotbot.com/

NAME   The HUMBUL Gateway
TYPE   Information server
PROVIDER   Oxford University Computing Service (UK)
DESCRIPTION   A gateway to international network resources for humanities scholars.
ACCESS
        URL(s)   http://info.ox.ac.uk/oucs/humanities/ international.html

NAME   Infoseek
TYPE   Searchable index; Information server
PROVIDER   Infoseek Corp. (USA)
DESCRIPTION   Combines a searchable database of web pages with a directory approach to resources by subject. Searching options go from basic to advanced with related concepts being suggested.
COMMENTS   At the time of writing a UK-specific version was offered.
ACCESS
        URL(s)   http://www2.infoseek.com

NAME   NISS Directory of Networked Resources
TYPE   Information server
PROVIDER   NISS (UK)
DESCRIPTION   Provides descriptions of, and access to information sources worldwide. Resources are arranged by UDC classification number, normally to the 2 digit level.
COMMENTS   In contrast to many subject listings, provides descriptions, written by subject experts, of resources. These descriptions are searchable by keyword.
ACCESS
        URL(s)   http://www.niss.ac.uk/subject/
        TELNET   niss.ac.uk
        PATH   Search the NISS Directory of Network resources
        LOGOUT   q

NAME PICK: quality Internet resources in library and information science, selected by Thomas Parry Library

TYPE Information server; Searchable index

PROVIDER Thomas Parry Library, University of Wales Aberystwyth

DESCRIPTION Contains selected resources organised in a subject directory structure. Keyword searching is available, as is a browsable listing in DDC 21 order.

ACCESS

> **URL(s)** http://www.aber.ac.uk/~tplwww/e/pick.html

NAME Search.com

TYPE Searchable index

PROVIDER CNET, Inc (USA)

DESCRIPTION Enormous list of links to other search services, directories etc, many of which are searchable from this site.

ACCESS

> **URL(s)** http://www.search.com/

NAME BUBL Search

TYPE Searchable indexes

PROVIDER BUBL Information Service (UK)

DESCRIPTION Provides for searching of BUBL files. Offers a good selection of searchable indexes for Internet resources generally and by category.

ACCESS

> **URL(s)** http://bubl.ac.uk/searches
> **TELNET** bubl.bath.ac.uk
> **LOGIN** bubl
> **PATH** BUBL Search
> **LOGOUT** q

NAME   **TradeWave Galaxy**
TYPE   Information server; Searchable index
PROVIDER   TradeWave Corp. (USA)
DESCRIPTION   An extensive subject listing of Internet services worldwide, including Web and other resources. Offers Boolean searching across subsets of resources WWW, gopher titles and telnet services. Search results are scored for relevance. Also provides links to subject indexes and major reference tools at other sites.
ACCESS
URL(s) http://www.einet.net/

NAME   **UK Index**
TYPE   Information server
PROVIDER   UK Index Limited (UK)
DESCRIPTION   Organises UK-based resources into general categories. Categories can be combined and keyword searched (with an AND option). A mailing list for notice of new entries in particular categories is available.
ACCESS
         URL(s)   http://www.ukindex.co.uk/

NAME   **Welcome to Lycos**
TYPE   Searchable index
PROVIDER   Lycos, Inc (USA)
DESCRIPTION   Indexes the texts of several million Web pages. Sounds and images from those pages are also searchable. Words and prefixes can be used as search terms. Boolean AND and NOT searching is offered.
ACCESS
         URL(s)   http://www-uk.lycos.com/

NAME   World Wide Web Virtual Library Subject Catalogue
TYPE   Information server
PROVIDER   W3C Consortium (International)
DESCRIPTION   A hierarchical subject index of Internet resources worldwide.
COMMENTS   The top menu contains an extensive listing of fairly specific subjects with an emphasis on the academic, though commercial, governmental, professional and recreational resources are also referenced. Most main subject headings link directly to other specialist sites maintained by volunteers. Some are disappointing; others very rich indeed.
ACCESS

> **URL(s)**   http://www.w3.org/pub/DataSources/bySubject/

NAME   WWLIB – Classified Listing of WWW Pages
TYPE   Information server
PROVIDER   Peter Burden
DESCRIPTION   Provides a classified listing of UK WWW pages.
COMMENTS   The classification (currently experimental) is broadly based on the 20th edition of Dewey, beginning at the single digit level on the home page. Section 0 (Generalities, Catalogues, Newspapers, Computing) and Section 3 (Social Sciences, Law, Government, Society, Commerce, Education) are particularly rich in UK Web sites that go well beyond the academic sector. Check Section 0 for servers provided by UK-based hardware and software companies, publishers and the media. Individual pages on the UK Government and H.M. Treasury servers are incorporated in Section 3, providing a useful resumé of what these cover. Also in Section 3, an extensive list of UK Internet service providers, and in Section 6 (Applied Science) a good collection of UK industrial companies with Web sites. This is a good resource to use for an overview of UK initiatives on the Web, a sort of Yahoo! equivalent for UK sites.
ACCESS

> **URL(s)**   http://www.scit.wlv.ac.uk/wwlib/

NAME   Yahoo!
TYPE   Information server; Searchable index
PROVIDER   Yahoo!, Inc (USA)
DESCRIPTION   An extensive and rapidly growing subject tree of WWW sites, beginning with a top level menu of about 20 broad subject headings. Most resources are described briefly. There is also a search facility for words and sub strings in titles, URLs and Comments   on the server. Yahoo! is also available in a number of national versions (there is one for the UK). Yahooligans! is a version of Yahoo! designed for children.
ACCESS

　　　　URL(S)　　　http://www.yahoo.co.uk/
　　　　　　　　　　　http://www.yahoo.com/

NAME   YELL, Yellow Pages UK Home Page
TYPE   Information server; Searchable index
PROVIDER   Yellow Pages Division of British Telecommunications PLC
DESCRIPTION   Mixture of directory and search service for UK resources. As well as web pages, also includes a searchable Electronic Yellow Pages, a UK Film Finder, a UK Company Directory and more.
ACCESS

　　　　URL(S)　　　http://www.yell.co.uk

OPACs and Library-Based Information Servers

NAME   **CARL Corporation**
TYPE   Information server
PROVIDER   The CARL Corporation (USA)
DESCRIPTION   Access to over 450 public, academic and school libraries in the USA plus links to a number of commercial databases (subscribers only), including the massive UnCover (journal contents) database.
ACCESS

URL(s)	http://www.carl.org/
TELNET	database.carl.org
LOGOUT	//EXIT

NAME   **Conservation OnLine**
TYPE   Information server
PROVIDER   Stanford University Libraries, Preservation Department (USA)
DESCRIPTION   Documents, mailing list archives and resources of relevance to the conservation of library, archives and museum materials.
ACCESS

URL(s)	http://palimpsest.stanford.edu/

NAME   **COPAC**
TYPE   OPAC
PROVIDER   COPAC Project, Manchester Computing, University of Manchester
DESCRIPTION   At the time of writing, the COPAC database contains around 3.5 million records from Cambridge, Oxford, Edinburgh, Glasgow and Leeds University libraries. More university collections will be added.
ACCESS

URL(s)	http://copac.ac.uk/copac/

NAME   **Digital Libraries: Cataloguing and Indexing of Electronic Resources**
TYPE   Information server
PROVIDER   International Federation of Library Associations (Canada)
DESCRIPTION   Provides links to relevant documents and other resources that deal with the cataloguing and indexing of electronic media.
ACCESS

URL(s)	http://ifla.inist.fr/II/catalog.htm
	http://www.nlc-bnc.ca/ifla/II/catalog.htm

NAME   **Hytelnet**
TYPE   Information server; Software archive
PROVIDER   Peter Scott (Canada)
DESCRIPTION   Hytelnet provides telnet addresses and links to Internet sites worldwide – predominantly academic library catalogues, but also some CWIS, freenets, bulletin boards, electronic books and other databases, Archie, Gopher and WWW servers, WHOIS, white page and directory services. OPACs are listed by geographical area and also by system (BLCMP, GEAC, Libertas, etc. etc.) and there are brief instructions for searching each system.
COMMENTS   Hytelnet is available in two forms, either as a service accessible via a web browser/telnet or as a piece of software which connects to resources itself. The software version is available via FTP for use on a local PC, Mac, VMS or Unix machine. Full instructions for download-ing and using the software on the Lights web server below.
ACCESS
      URL(S)   http://www.cam.ac.uk/Hytelnet/
                             http://moondog.usask.ca/hytelnet/
      TELNET   info.mcc.ac.uk
                             130.88.203.16
      LOGIN   hytelnet
ACCESS (SOFTWARE VERSION)
      URL(S)   http://www.lights.com/hytelnet/
                             ftp://ftp.usask.ca/pub/hytelnet/

NAME   **Innovative Internet Applications in Libraries**
TYPE   Information server
PROVIDER   Ken Middleton, Middle Tennessee State University (USA)
DESCRIPTION   Provides links to well-chosen examples of library use of the Internet for a wealth of activities, including bibliographic instruction, cat-aloguing, collection management, library tours, digital library and elec-tronic publishing projects, public relations and more. Includes some references to relevant publications and examples of Web forms for book requests, inter-library loans and OPAC searches.
COMMENTS   A source of inspiration for libraries who are planning Internet services.
ACCESS
      URL(S)   http://frank.mtsu.edu/~kmiddlet/libweb/
                             innovate.html

NAME The Internet Public Library
TYPE Information server
PROVIDER School of Information and Library Studies, University of Michigan (USA)
DESCRIPTION Provides services for children and young people plus links to Internet resources (mostly US) chosen for their interest to public librarians and users. Incorporates an experimental 'ask a question' service for reference questions submitted via e-mail and "rooms" that can be visited.
COMMENTS Available in graphical and text-only versions. An imaginative experimental concept.
ACCESS
  URL(s)   http://ipl.sils.umich.edu/

NAME LASER
TYPE Information server
PROVIDER LASER – London and South Eastern Library Region (UK)
DESCRIPTION Brief information about this library co-operative and associated services and projects, for example VISCOUNT (interlending and bibliographic records), CILLA (acquisition and cataloguing of ethnic language materials) etc.
ACCESS
  URL(s)   http://lirn.viscount.org.uk/laser/

NAME Library of Congress Home Page
TYPE Information server
PROVIDER Library of Congress (USA)
DESCRIPTION Information at and about the Library of Congress, including a link to the LOCIS catalogue and details of how to search it. Also US government, legislative and congressional information and resources for librarians, information professionals and researchers.
ACCESS
  URL(s)   http://lcweb.loc.gov/homepage/

NAME Online Catalogs with 'Webbed' Interfaces
TYPE Information server
PROVIDER Eric Lease Morgan, North Carolina State University (USA)
DESCRIPTION Gives examples of catalogues with 'built in' Web interfaces, "bolted-on" Web interfaces (to existing catalogues) and Web to Z39.50 gateways.
COMMENTS Some useful ideas for those designing Web interfaces for OPACs.
ACCESS

URL(s) http://www.lib.ncsu.edu/staff/morgan/alcuin/
wwwed-catalogs.html

NAME Libweb
TYPE Information server
PROVIDER Thomas Dowling, University of Washington (USA)
DESCRIPTION A well organised list of library-based Web servers from around the world. Also includes a few library-related companies (online service, database and bibliographic software providers).
COMMENTS Includes useful library Web servers from the UK, and a good selection from Northern Europe. These give links to OPACs and a wealth of other resources.
ACCESS

URL(s) http://sunsite.berkeley.edu/Libweb/

NAME LOCIS – Library of Congress Information System
TYPE OPAC
PROVIDER Library of Congress (USA)
DESCRIPTION The Library of Congress main catalogue of books and other materials (approaching 30 million records in over 400 languages) plus five other special collections.
ACCESS

TELNET locis.loc.gov
140.147.254.3
LOGOUT 12

NAME   Portico
TYPE   Information server
PROVIDER   The British Library (UK)
DESCRIPTION   Online information about the British Library, principally details of BL structure, functions, events, services and collections and (additionally) information about digitisation and networking projects, forthcoming exhibitions etc. Includes a link to GABRIEL, the web server for Europe's national libraries.
ACCESS

      URL(s)   http://www.bl.uk/
                     http://portico.bl.uk/

NAME   Project EARL
TYPE   Information server
PROVIDER   EARL
DESCRIPTION   EARL is a consortium of UK Public Library authorities and other organisations which aim to make available the Internet to all library users.
ACCESS

      URL(s)   http://www.viscount.org.uk/

NAME   RLG Home Page
TYPE   Information server
PROVIDER   Research Libraries Group, Inc. (USA)
DESCRIPTION   Information from the RLG and links to Web servers at member institutions.
ACCESS

      URL(s)   http://www.rlg.org/

NAME   SALSER – Scottish Academic Library Serials
TYPE   Information server
PROVIDER   SCURL – Scottish Confederation of University and Research Libraries (UK)
DESCRIPTION   A catalogue of journals and other serials held in Scotland's university libraries, the City Libraries of Edinburgh and Glasgow, and the National Library of Scotland. Telnet links are also provided to Scottish university OPACs.
COMMENTS   Useful for locating which libraries in a specified region hold a particular journal. Users first select sites before searching by exact journal title, keyword (Boolean) or ISSN. Searches return holdings information.
ACCESS
    URL(S)   http://edina.ed.ac.uk/salser/

NAME   Technical Processing Tools Online (TPOT)
TYPE   Information server
PROVIDER   George J. Janczym, UCSD Libraries (USA)
DESCRIPTION   An impressive guide to web resources for acquisitions, cataloguing and serials processing.
ACCESS
    URL(S)   http://tpot.ucsd.edu/

NAME   UK Higher Education Library Catalogues
TYPE   Information server
PROVIDER   NISS (UK)
DESCRIPTION   Lists OPACs of higher education and research institutions in the UK. Gives contact, login and basic search instructions for each OPAC and also provides links through to the majority.
ACCESS
    URL(S)   http://www.niss.ac.uk/reference/opacs.html
    TELNET   niss.ac.uk
    PATH   Reference and bibliographic/Library OPACS/ Higher Education and Research

NAME   Web4Lib

TYPE   Discussion list (moderated)

PROVIDER   Information Systems Instruction and Support, University of California Berkeley Library (USA)

DESCRIPTION   Aimed at librarians who are involved in the creation and management of library-based Web servers and clients.

ACCESS

    URL(S)   http://sunsite.berkeley.edu/Web4Lib/

SUBSCRIPTION DETAILS

    E-MAIL   listserv@library.berkeley.edu

    MESSAGE   subscribe web4lib *your-firstname your-lastname*

Resources from other organizations

BOOKSELLERS, PUBLISHERS AND THE MEDIA

NAME   The BBC Home Page

TYPE   Information server

PROVIDER   BBC – British Broadcasting Corporation (UK)

DESCRIPTION   TV and Radio programme schedules; programme information, factsheets and some transcripts; current affairs; news reviews and analysis; BBC Education resources; and much more from and about the BBC.

ACCESS

    URL(s)   http://www.bbc.co.uk/

NAME   Book Industry Communication's Bookish Home Page

TYPE   Information server

PROVIDER   Book Industry Communication (UK)

DESCRIPTION   A central access point for information from the UK book industry plus links to relevant international sites. Includes UK and Irish booksellers, library suppliers, subscription agents, library systems suppliers, UK and European English language publishers who are providing information via the network.

ACCESS

    URL(s)   http://www.bic.org.uk/bic/

NAME   Book Web Home Page

TYPE   Information server

PROVIDER   American Booksellers Association (USA)

DESCRIPTION   News, discussion and information about books, authors and the U.S. book industry.

ACCESS

    URL(s)   http://www.ambook.org/

NAME   **BUBL LINK: 070.5 Publishing**
TYPE   Information server
PROVIDER   BUBL Information Service (UK)
DESCRIPTION   A collection of links to booksellers and publishers (conventional and electronic), both US and UK.
ACCESS

URL(S)	http://link.bubl.ac.uk/publishing/
TELNET	bubl.bath.ac.uk
LOGIN	bubl
PATH	BUBL Link/Browse by Subject/P/Publishing and Bookselling

NAME   **The Daily News – just the links**
TYPE   Information server
PROVIDER   Gerben Vos, Vrije University (Netherlands)
DESCRIPTION   Provides extensive links to European and worldwide news and weather services on the Internet.
ACCESS

URL(S)	http://www.cs.vu.nl/~gerben/news.html

NAME   **IBIC – Internet Book Information Center**
TYPE   Information server
PROVIDER   SunSITE at University of North Carolina (USA)
DESCRIPTION   Provides good links to a wealth of (mostly US) publishing and bookselling resources on the Internet, including awards and bestsellers, author information, book reviews, poetry archives, USENET newsgroups as well as directories of publishers and booksellers themselves.
ACCESS

URL(S)	http://sunsite.unc.edu/ibic/

NAME   Internet Bookshop Homepage
TYPE   Information server
PROVIDER   The Internet Book Shop (UK)
DESCRIPTION   Claimed to be the largest online bookshop in the world.
   Includes Whitaker's 'Books in Print' (keyword searching on title, author,
   publisher or ISBN); catalogues from about 20 publishers (general and
   specialist); a subject tree to browse titles from the listed publishers; links
   to home pages of bookshops around the world.
ACCESS
      URL(s)   http://www.bookshop.co.uk/

NAME   Media UK Internet Directory
TYPE   Information server
PROVIDER   Media UK
DESCRIPTION   E-mail contact addresses and links to UK media-related sites
   including TV, radio, newspapers (local and national) and magazines.
ACCESS
      URL(s)   http://www.mediauk.com/directory/

NAME   Publishers' Catalogues Home Page
TYPE   Information server
PROVIDER   Peter Scott, Northern Lights Internet Solutions Ltd. (Canada)
DESCRIPTION   Publishers' information servers and catalogues from around
   the world, listed by country.
ACCESS
      URL(s)   http://www.lights.com/publisher/

NAME   The World-Wide Web Virtual Library: Publishers
TYPE   Information server
PROVIDER   Jonathan Bowen, Oxford University Computing Laboratory
   (UK)
DESCRIPTION   An extensive alphabetical list of Internet-accessible publishers
   from around the world. Also provides links to selected online bookstores
   and to broadcasters (listed by country).
ACCESS
      URL(s)   http://www.comlab.ox.ac.uk/archive/publishers.
            html

Commercial Online Information Retrieval Services

Name BIDS

Type Information server; Online retrieval service

Provider BIDS – Bath Information and Data Services (UK)

Description BIDS supports end-user access to a number of commercial online bibliographic databases, principally the ISI Citation Indexes, the British Library Document Supply Centre's Inside Information database, CARL Corporation's UnCover (journal contents) and several subject-specific bibliographic databases.

Comments Information about the service and databases is available on the Web server. Although established for UK academic institutions, subscriptions to some of the databases are available more widely. There is a Mailbase discussion list for BIDS users (lis-bids-users).

Access

URL(s)	http://www.bids.ac.uk/
Telnet	bids.ac.uk (subscribers only)
	193.63.84.10

Contact details

E-mail	bidshelp@bath.ac.uk
Tel	01225-826074
Fax	01225-826176

Name Blaise Web

Type Information server; Online retrieval service

Provider The British Library (UK)

Description Hosts the major British Library catalogues and MARC files as well as related databases from other suppliers.

Comments Service information is posted to the lis-bl-blaiseline list on Mailbase.

Access

URL(S)	http://blaiseweb.bl.uk/
Telnet	blaise.bl.uk (subscribers only)
	194.216.12.1

Contact details

E-mail	blaiseline-helpdesk@bl.uk

NAME   DataStar Web
TYPE   Information server; Online retrieval service
PROVIDER   Knight-Ridder Information (USA)
DESCRIPTION   A multidisciplinary online host, but with an emphasis on healthcare, biomedical, biotechnology and business information. The server provides brief, keyword-searchable descriptions of all DataStar databases, listed by their codes.
ACCESS

URL(s)	http://www.krinfo.ch/krinfo/products/dsweb/
TELNET	rserve.rs.ch (subscribers only)
	192.82.124.34

NAME   DIMDI
TYPE   Online retrieval service
PROVIDER   DIMDI (Germany)
DESCRIPTION   Offers a wide range of databases in the health, biological and related sciences.
ACCESS

TELNET	dimdi.x29-gw.dfn.de (subscribers only)
	129.143.3.20

NAME   European Community Host Organisation – ECHO
TYPE   Information server; Online retrieval service
PROVIDER   ECHO – European Community Host Organisation (Europe)
DESCRIPTION   A non-commercial host, offering access to a number of databases from the EU covering European Community R&D, industry, the economy and the language industry.
ACCESS

URL(s)	http://www2.echo.lu/echo/en/menuecho.html
TELNET	echo.lu
	193.91.44.130
LOGIN	echo
LOGOUT	90/5/3
NOTE	A limited free service is available but users must register to use the full service.

CONTACT DETAILS

TEL	0800-899256 (freephone)

NAME   **European Patent Office**
TYPE   Information server
PROVIDER   European Patent Office (Austria)
DESCRIPTION   Information from and about the EPO (e.g. patent granting procedures), links to servers from other Patent Offices around the world, plus details of commercial databases containing patent information.
ACCESS
  URL(S)   http://www.austria.eu.net/epo/

NAME   **ESA/IRS**
TYPE   Online retrieval service
PROVIDER   European Space Agency Information Retrieval Service (Italy)
DESCRIPTION   Predominantly scientific and technical databases.
ACCESS
  TELNET   esrin.esa.it (subscribers only)
                    192.106.252.1

NAME   **ISO Online**
TYPE   Information server
PROVIDER   ISO – International Standards Organisation (Switzerland)
DESCRIPTION   Includes information about ISO, its structure, membership and activities. Makes freely available a catalogue of all ISO standards (including drafts), handbooks and other publications.
COMMENTS   Standards are listed by subject according to the International Classification for Standards. The catalogue can also be searched by text keyword and standard number. Pricing and ordering information is available, although online ordering is not supported.
ACCESS
  URL(S)   http://www.iso.ch/

NAME   Knight-Ridder Information Web Site
TYPE   Information server; Online retrieval service
PROVIDER   Knight-Ridder Information (USA)
DESCRIPTION   There are hundreds of databases on Knight-Ridder's Dialog, covering all disciplines. Information about both online and Ondisc (CD-ROM) information products and services, including associated publications, such as the Dialog Database Catalog and Price List, are available on the server. Database descriptions can be browsed by subject or searched by keyword.
COMMENTS   Dialog news and updates are also distributed to subscribers of the majordomo@www.dialog.com mailing list.
ACCESS

URL(s)	http://www.dialog.com/
TELNET	dialog.com (subscribers only)
	192.132.3.252

CONTACT DETAILS

E-MAIL	info@www.dialog.com

NAME   LEXIS-NEXIS Communication Center
TYPE   Information server; Online retrieval service
PROVIDER   LEXIS-NEXIS (USA)
DESCRIPTION   News and legal information from the USA and around the world. The server includes (amongst others) a guide to system commands, an alphabetical list of Lexis/Nexis files.
ACCESS

URL(s)	http://www.lexis-nexis.com/
TELNET	nex.lexis-nexis.com (subscribers only)
	192.73.216.260

NAME   N2K Telebase
TYPE   Information server; Online retrieval service
PROVIDER   Telebase Systems (USA)
DESCRIPTION   Offers access to around 250 online databases including many well known business sources. Subscription details are available on the server, as well as brief database descriptions.
ACCESS

URL(s)	http://www.telebase.com/
TELNET	easynet.telebase.com (subscribers only)
	192.132.57.2

CONTACT DETAILS

E-MAIL	info@telebase.com

NAME   **NlightN Home Page**
TYPE   Information server; Online retrieval service
PROVIDER   NlightN (USA)
DESCRIPTION   Offers access to around 300 online databases as well as web pages, USENET newsgroups etc. Interesting for its mixture of traditional and Internet sources. Subscription details are available on the server.
ACCESS
URL(S)   http://www.nlightn.com/

NAME   **OCLC – Online Computer Library Centre**
TYPE   Information server; Online retrieval service
PROVIDER   OCLC – Online Computer Library Centre, Inc. (USA)
DESCRIPTION   OCLC First Search provides access to OCLC's online union catalogue of member libraries (World Cat), other OCLC databases and some well-known databases from other suppliers. Information and limited OCLC documentation available on the server.
ACCESS
URL(S)   http://www.oclc.org/
TELNET   fscat.oclc.org (subscribers only)
204.151.6.110

NAME   **SilverPlatter Worldwide Library**
TYPE   Information server
PROVIDER   Silver Platter Information, Inc. (USA and International)
DESCRIPTION   Details of Silver Platter's CD-ROM and related information products, training and support services, software and Internet-related activities.
ACCESS
URL(S)   http://www.silverplatter.com/
ftp://ftp.silverplatter.com/

NAME   **STN International**
TYPE   Information server; Online retrieval service
PROVIDER   STN – Scientific and Technical Information Network (Germany)
DESCRIPTION   Over 100 scientific and technical databases with a strong emphasis on chemical information.
ACCESS
URL(S)   http://www.fiz-karlsruhe.de/stn.html
TELNET   stn.fiz-karlsruhe.de (subscribers only)
141.66.16.239

NAME UMI: the Answer Company

TYPE Information server

PROVIDER UMI Inc (USA)

DESCRIPTION UMI provides bibliographic, microfilming and distribution services for doctoral and master's theses and dissertations produced worldwide. There is a wealth of information and guidelines about the dissertations services on both servers. Additionally the Web server contains information about additional UMI products, services and events including document delivery, electronic products and serials on microform.

ACCESS

    URL(S)   http://www.umi.com/

NAME UnCover

TYPE Alerting service; Document delivery service; Online retrieval service

PROVIDER CARL Corporation (USA); BH Blackwell Group (UK)

DESCRIPTION Offers tables of contents and a document delivery service for approximately 17,000 journals. Providing multi-disciplinary and international journal coverage, this is one of the largest and most up-to-date databases of its kind.

COMMENTS Documents can be ordered online and delivered by fax. Contents pages of selected journals can be delivered to individuals' electronic mail boxes. There is a fee for this and for every document ordered, but no charge for searching the database (by author, keyword or journal title). Further information about UnCover and other CARL services is available on the Web server. Use telnet to connect directly to the database. (UK academic libraries normally access via the BIDS subscription service).

ACCESS

    URL(S)   http://www.carl.org/uncover/unchome.html

    TELNET   database.carl.org

    PATH   1: Uncover

    LOGOUT   //EXIT

CONTACT DETAILS

    E-MAIL   uncover@blackwell.co.uk

    TEL   01865-261362

155

GOVERNMENT, GOVERNMENT-RELATED AND INTERNATIONAL ORGANIZATIONS

NAME   British Politics Page
TYPE   Information server
PROVIDER   Julian White, Politics Department, Keele University
DESCRIPTION   Provides a complete alphabetical index of all parties, constituencies, councils etc.
ACCESS

> **URL(s)**   http://www.keele.ac.uk/depts/po/table/brit/
> brit.htm

NAME   CCTA Government Information Service
TYPE   Information server
PROVIDER   CCTA – Central Computer and Telecommunications Authority (UK)
DESCRIPTION   Acts as a repository for information supplied by a large number of UK government departments and agencies, with links to those who have their own information servers (mostly Web sites). These range from the Central Office of Information to the Charity Commission, the British Council to the Building Research Establishment. The full texts of citizen's charters are rapidly being added as is information from local government as it becomes available.
COMMENTS   Departments and organisations are listed by name and by function (e.g. Agriculture, Careers). There is also a keyword search facility.
ACCESS

> **URL(s)**   http://www.open.gov.uk/

NAME   CORDIS Homepage
TYPE   Information server
PROVIDER   European Union (EC)
DESCRIPTION   Information on all EU-supported research and development activities including programmes, publications and research partnerships.
ACCESS

> **URL(s)**   http://www.cordis.lu/
> **TELNET**   echo.lu
> 193.91.44.130
> **LOGIN**   echo
> **LOGOUT**   90/5/3

NAME   ERSC RAPID: Research Activities and Publications
Information Database
TYPE   Directory
PROVIDER   Edinburgh University, for the Economic and Social Research
Council (UK)
DESCRIPTION   Records of all ESRC-funded research awards since April 1985
and resulting publications of all types (including conventional publica-
tions, audio-visual, software and datasets).
ACCESS

URL(s)	http://edina.ed.ac.uk/rapid/
TELNET	ercvax.ed.ac.uk
LOGIN	RAPID
PASSWORD	RAPID
LOGOUT	Q

NAME   EUROPA
TYPE   Information server
PROVIDER   European Commission (EC)
DESCRIPTION   Information on the European Union's goals, institutions and
policies.
ACCESS

URL(s)	http://europa.eu.int/

NAME   Europe and the Global Information Society – Bangemann
Report
TYPE   Full text document
PROVIDER   Bangemann Commission (EC)
DESCRIPTION   Recommendations made in 1994 to the European Council on
measures to be considered for developing European-wide information
infrastructures.
ACCESS

URL(s)	http://www.earn.net/EC/bangemann.html

NAME   FedWorld Information Network
TYPE   Information server
PROVIDER   NTIS – National Technical Information Service (USA)
DESCRIPTION   US Government information servers, FTP, Gopher and tel-
net sites organised by subject. Also reports, databases and software from
NTIS.
ACCESS

URL(s)	http://www.fedworld.gov/
	ftp://ftp.fedworld.gov

NAME   I*M – Europe Home Page
TYPE   Information server
PROVIDER   DG XIII (EC)
DESCRIPTION   Information about the EU and European Parliament, notably EU programmes and calls for proposals related to the European information market and the IMPACT programme.
ACCESS

URL(s)	http://www.echo.lu/
TELNET	echo.lu
LOGIN	echo

NAME   REFLAW: The Virtual Reference & Legal & Government & Politics
TYPE   Information server
PROVIDER   Washburn University School of Law Library, Kansas (USA)
DESCRIPTION   Predominantly US government, political and legal information but some useful links to international resources too, including GATT, UN, Nato treaties and agreements and US foreign affairs news.
ACCESS

URL(s)	http://law.wuacc.edu/washlaw/reflaw/reflaw.html

NAME   UNDP – Development Programme
TYPE   Information server
PROVIDER   United Nations (International)
DESCRIPTION   UN documents, conferences, directories etc.
ACCESS

URL(s)	http://www.undp.org/

NAME Worldwide Government and Public Administration Resources
TYPE   Information server
PROVIDER   SOSIG (UK)
DESCRIPTION   Links to Internet-accessible government servers worldwide.
ACCESS

URL(s)	http://sosig.ac.uk/Subjects/govt.html
TELNET	sosig.ac.uk
LOGIN	sosig
PATH	Worldwide Resources/Government and Public Administration

Library and Information Education

NAME **BAILER WWW Server**
TYPE Information server
PROVIDER British Association for Information and Library Education and Research (UK)
DESCRIPTION Includes information from and about BAILER and its committees, and a directory of UK Departments of Library and Information Studies. Also contains links to directories of LIS departments in other parts of the world.
ACCESS
      URL(s) http://epip.lboro.ac.uk/bailer/

NAME **CRISTAL-ED**
TYPE Information server, Discussion list
PROVIDER School of Information and Library Studies, University of Michigan (USA)
DESCRIPTION Information from a five-year project (commencing 1995) which aims to 'reinvent' the core curriculum for ILS to meet changing needs and to define new ILS specialisations.
ACCESS
      URL(s) http://www.si.umich.edu/cristaled/
SUBSCRIPTION DETAILS
      E-MAIL majordomo@si.umich.edu
      MESSAGE subscribe cristal-ed

NAME **CTI Home Page**
TYPE Information server
PROVIDER CTI – Computers in Teaching Initiative (UK)
DESCRIPTION The CTI is funded by the Higher Education Funding Councils and provides information and support on the use of computers for teaching in HE via a number of specialist centres dealing with different disciplines (of which Library and Information Studies is one). The server provides general information from CTI headquarters, including events and publications, and links to all the various subject centres.
ACCESS
      URL(s) http://www.cti.ac.uk

Name   CTILIS Home Page
TYPE   Information server
PROVIDER   Computers in Teaching Initiative, Centre for Library and Information Studies (UK)
DESCRIPTION   The server carries (mostly) back issues of newsletters from CTILIS, the contents of which include reviews and reports of software packages used in teaching. Also links to other resources for LIS educators.
ACCESS
          URL(S)   http://info.lboro.ac.uk/departments/ls/cti/

NAME   ITTI – Home Page
TYPE   Information server, Directory
PROVIDER   ITTI – Information Technology Training Initiative (UK)
DESCRIPTION   ITTI is funded by the Higher Education Funding Councils to support the development of IT training materials, which are listed on this service.
COMMENTS   Aimed at the HE sector but of likely interest to others involved in IT training.
ACCESS
          URL(S)   http://www.hull.ac.uk/Hull/ITTI/

NAME   JESSE
TYPE   Discussion list
PROVIDER   Gretchen Whitney, University of Tennessee (USA)
DESCRIPTION   An open forum for discussion of library and information science education.
COMMENTS   Almost all postings are from the USA.
SUBSCRIPTION DETAILS
          E-MAIL   listserv@utkvm1.utk.edu
          MESSAGE   subscribe jesse *your-firstname your-lastname*

NAME   The Katherine Sharp Review
TYPE   Electronic journal (refereed)
ISSN   1083-5261
PROVIDER   Graduate School of Library and Information Science, University of Illinois (USA)
DESCRIPTION   Publishes articles within the field of library and information science from student authors.
ACCESS
          URL(S)   http://edfu.lis.uiuc.edu/review/

NAME   LIS-BAILER
TYPE   Discussion list (unmoderated)
PROVIDER   BAILER – British Association for Information and Library Education and Research (UK)
DESCRIPTION   Aimed at lecturers and research staff in Departments of Library and Information Studies.
ACCESS
      URL(s)   http://www.mailbase.ac.uk/lists/lis-bailer/
SUBSCRIPTION DETAILS
      E-MAIL   mailbase@mailbase.ac.uk
      MESSAGE   join lis-bailer *your-firstname your-lastname*

NAME   LIS Schools on the Net
TYPE   Information server
PROVIDER   Internet Training and Consultancy Services (USA)
DESCRIPTION   Links to Web servers in (predominantly) US library and information schools, but also a few international.
COMMENTS   For UK schools, use the BAILER WWW Server.
ACCESS
      URL(s)   http://www.itcs.com/topten/libschools.html

NAME   LISSPS – Library and Information Studies Students and Prospective Students
TYPE   Information server; Discussion list
PROVIDER   Andrew Brown and UKOLN
DESCRIPTION   An information server and discussion list aimed at students on LIS courses and those intending to apply for one.
ACCESS
      URL(s)   http://ukoln.bath.ac.uk/lissps/
SUBSCRIPTION DETAILS
      E-MAIL   majordomo@ukoln.bath.ac.uk
      MESSAGE   subscribe lissps

NAME NCET Home Page

TYPE Information server

PROVIDER NCET – Council for Educational Technology (UK)

DESCRIPTION A wealth of information on educational technology including NCET publications and project details. Also provides links to other education-specific information servers (mostly UK).

COMMENTS A highly functional menu structure allows access to information by user orientation/needs. This includes access by user's role (e.g. parent/librarian); educational level (e.g. primary/secondary); specific subject (e.g. GNVQs); Type of technology (e.g. computer software) etc.

ACCESS

      URL(s)   http://www.ncet.org.uk/

NAME The Times Higher Internet Service Type Alerting service

TYPE Information server

PROVIDER The Times Higher Education Supplement (UK)

DESCRIPTION Headlines, introductions, digests and summaries of items in the current issue only of the newspaper. Also includes job advertisements (before the Friday paper), booklists and mailing lists for topical discussions.

ACCESS

      URL(s)   http://www.timeshigher.newsint.co.uk/

LIS AND RELATED PROFESSIONAL ASSOCIATIONS

NAME   **American Library Association Home Page**
TYPE   Information server
PROVIDER   American Library Association (USA)
DESCRIPTION   Information about the membership, constitution, activities, publications etc. of the ALA. Policy and consultative documents available.
ACCESS
> **URL(s)**   http://www.ala.org/

NAME   **ARL Web Server**
TYPE   Information server
PROVIDER   Association of Research Libraries (USA)
DESCRIPTION   ARL membership list, reports and publications.
ACCESS
> **URL(s)**   http://arl.cni.org/

NAME   **BCS Net**
TYPE   Information server
PROVIDER   British Computer Society (UK)
DESCRIPTION   BCS structure, events, awards, publications, etc.
ACCESS
> **URL(s)**   http://www.bcs.org.uk/

NAME   **IEE Home Page**
TYPE   Information server
PROVIDER   Institution of Electrical Engineers (UK)
DESCRIPTION   Professional, publishing and information services from the IEE.
ACCESS
> **URL(s)**   http://www.iee.org.uk/

NAME   IFLANET
TYPE   Information server
PROVIDER   IFLA – International Federation of Library Associations (Canada
    & Netherlands)
DESCRIPTION   The service began with information about IFLA (structure,
    membership, publications, grants, conferences etc.) but, on the Web
    server, is now adding compilations of other documents and resources of
    generic interest to the library world including copyright and intellectual
    property; cataloguing and indexing of electronic resources; interlibrary
    loan, document delivery and resource sharing information; IT standards
    and organisations; and library and related information policy statements.
ACCESS
    URL(s)   http://ifla.inist.fr/
              http://www.nlc-bnc.ca/ifla/

NAME   Institute of Information Scientists
TYPE   Information server
PROVIDER   The Institute of Information Scientists (UK)
DESCRIPTION   Information about the Institute, its newsletter Inform, how to
    become a member etc.
ACCESS
    URL(s)   http://www.dcs.gla.ac.uk/IIS/

NAME   The Library Association
TYPE   Information server
PROVIDER   The Library Association (UK)
DESCRIPTION   Information about events, training courses etc, including LA
    Branches and special interest Groups. Also includes a regularly updated
    Web page for Library Association Publishing, including a full list of pub-
    lications, author information and book reviews.
ACCESS
    URL(s)   http://www.fdgroup.co.uk/la.htm

NAME   **LIS-FID**
TYPE   Information server; Discussion list (unmoderated)
PROVIDER   Staff of Queen Margaret College, Edinburgh on behalf of the International Federation for Information and Documentation (Netherlands)
DESCRIPTION   Aims to promote discussion of information management and library and information science in an international context.
ACCESS
      URL(s)   http://www.mailbase.ac.uk/lists/lis-fid/
SUBSCRIPTION DETAILS
      E-MAIL   mailbase@mailbase.ac.uk
      MESSAGE   join lis-fid *your-firstname your-lastname*

NAME   **LIS-IIS**
TYPE   Information server; Discussion list (unmoderated)
PROVIDER   Members of the Institute of Information Scientists (UK)
DESCRIPTION   This list is open to anyone interested in discussing information science issues.
ACCESS
      URL(s)   http://www.mailbase.ac.uk/lists/lis-iis/
SUBSCRIPTION DETAILS
      E-MAIL   mailbase@mailbase.ac.uk
      MESSAGE   join lis-iis *your-firstname your-lastname*

NAME   **SIGIR Information Server**
TYPE   Information server
PROVIDER   Association for Computing Machinery – Special Interest Group on Information Retrieval (USA)
DESCRIPTION   Information about ACM SIGIR plus links to a selection of other related SIGs, professional societies and resources.
ACCESS
      URL(s)   http://info.sigir.acm.org/sigir/

Resources linked to Part III

UTILITIES

NAME   Accessing the Internet by E-Mail: Doctor Bob's Guide to
Offline Internet Access
TYPE   Full text document
PROVIDER   Bob Rankin (USA)
DESCRIPTION   How to access FTP, Gopher, Archie, Veronica, Finger,
USENET, WHOIS, Netfind, WAIS and the World Wide Web via e-mail.
COMMENTS   E-mail access is no substitute for the "real thing" but this gives
valuable guidance if e-mail is all you have.
ACCESS

E-MAIL	mailbase@mailbase.ac.uk
MESSAGE	send lis-iis e-access-inet.txt

NAME   Anonymous Surfing
TYPE   Information server
PROVIDER   Community ConneXion, Inc. (USA)
DESCRIPTION   Removes the information that browsers offer about their
users. Also contains links to other sites related to security.
ACCESS

URL(S)   http://www.anonymizer.com/

NAME   Anonymous Remailers
TYPE   Full text document
PROVIDER   Andre Bacard (USA)
DESCRIPTION   FAQ (regularly posted to news.answers) which provides a
clear explanation of remailers, and includes a reference to a list of reliable
remailers.
ACCESS

URL(S)	http://www.cs.berkeley.edu/~raph/ remailer-faq.html
E-MAIL	abacard@well.sf.ca.us
SUBJECT	send FAQs info
MESSAGE	none needed

NAME   BrowserWatch – Plug-In Plaza
TYPE   Information server
PROVIDER   World (USA)
DESCRIPTION   Lists web browser plug-ins both by type and computer plat-
form.
ACCESS

URL(S)   http://browserwatch.iworld.com/plug-in.html

NAME   **Cryptography, PGP and your Privacy**
TYPE   Information server
PROVIDER   Francis Litterio (USA)
DESCRIPTION   An exhaustive compilation of information relating to the important area of cryptographic applications for networks. Contains details on where to get the PGP (Pretty Good Privacy) package and how to use it. Part of the WWW Virtual Library.
ACCESS
        URL(s)   http://world.std.com/~franl/crypto.html

NAME   **Deja News – Post Newsgroup Article**
TYPE   Information server
PROVIDER   Deja News, Inc (USA)
DESCRIPTION   Gives two methods to post to a USENET newsgroup, one involving personal registration, the other confirming posts one by one.
ACCESS
        URL(s)   http://www.dejanews.com/post.xp

NAME **HyperText Markup Language (HTML): Working and Background Materials**
TYPE   Information server
PROVIDER   W3C Consortium
DESCRIPTION   Includes an explanation of HTML markup tags plus details of the development of HTML.
ACCESS
        URL(s)   http://www.w3.org/pub/WWW/MarkUp/

NAME   **The Jargon File**
TYPE   Information server
PROVIDER   Eric S. Raymond
DESCRIPTION A well-organised list of jargon used by computer sub-cultures. Contains links to related documents on hackers and hacking.
ACCESS
        URL(s)   http://www.ccil.org/jargon/

NAME   Multimedia File Formats on the Internet
TYPE   Information server
PROVIDER   Allison Zhang (USA)
DESCRIPTION   Encyclopaedic guide to PC file types, file compression/de-
compression and viewer/player software. Contains links to the actual soft-
ware.
ACCESS:

    URL(s)   http://rodent.lib.rochester.edu/multimed/
             contents.htm

NAME   The Net: User Guidelines and Netiquette
TYPE   Full text document
PROVIDER   Arlene Rinaldi (USA)
DESCRIPTION   The http URL contains links to the above document in
HTML form and to related material on site computer use policies.
ACCESS

    URL(s)   http://www.fau.edu/rinaldi/netiquette.html
             ftp://ftp.lib.berkeley.edu/pub/net.training/
             FAU/netiquette.ps
             ftp://ftp.lib.berkeley.edu/pub/net.training/
             FAU/netiquette.txt
    E-MAIL   alamanac@esusda.giv
    MESSAGE   send docs-gen rinaldi-netiquette

NAME   Running a World-Wide Web Service
TYPE   Full text document
PROVIDER   Brian Kelly (UK)
DESCRIPTION   Covers the technical and procedural aspects of setting up a
Web service in depth, with some less detailed discussion of social, legal
and organisational issues.
COMMENTS   Uses predominantly UK examples. Brings together much
technical information available from otherwise disparate sources on the
Internet.
ACCESS

    URL(s)   http://info.mcc.ac.uk/MVC/SIMA/handbook/
             handbook.html

NAME   **The Unofficial Smiley Dictionary**
TYPE   Information server
PROVIDER   EFF – Electronic Frontier Foundation (USA)
DESCRIPTION   A long list of smileys (emoticons). Part of the 'EFFs' (Extended) Guide to the Internet'.
ACCESS

> **URL(s)**   http://ukoln.bath.ac.uk/mirror/dummy/web/
> eeg_286.html#SEC287
> http://www.eff.org/papers/eegtti/eeg_286.html
> #SEC287

NAME   **White Pages**
TYPE   Information server
PROVIDER   Yahoo!, Inc (USA)
DESCRIPTION   Gives a comprehensive list of services for looking up email addresses. Coverage of UK email addresses is still poor.
ACCESS

> **URL(s)**   http://www.yahoo.co.uk/Reference/White_Pages/
> http://www.yahoo.com/Reference/White_Pages/

NAME   **World-Wide Web FAQ**
TYPE   Information server
PROVIDER   Thomas Boutell and Boutell.Com, Inc (USA)
DESCRIPTION   Definitive guide to all thigns pertaining to World Wide Web.
ACCESS

> **URL(s)**   http://info.ox.ac.uk/help/wwwfaq/
> http://www.boutell.com/faq/

INDEX

Entries which appear in the Resource Guide are shown in *italics*